C

Programming and Coding Question Bank with Solutions

by

Swati Saxena

BPB PUBLICATIONS

Distributors:

BPB PUBLICATIONS
20, Ansari Road, Darya Ganj
New Delhi-110002
Ph: 23254990/23254991

BPB BOOK CENTRE
376 Old Lajpat Rai Market,
Delhi-110006
Ph: 23861747

DECCAN AGENCIES
4-3-329, Bank Street,
Hyderabad-500195
Ph: 24756967/24756400

MICRO MEDIA
Shop No. 5, Mahendra Chambers, 150
DN Rd. Next to Capital Cinema, V.T.
(C.S.T.) Station, MUMBAI-400 001 Ph:
22078296/22078297

COMPUTER BOOK CENTRE
12, Shrungar Shopping Centre,
M.G.Road, BENGALURU–560001
Ph: 25587923/25584641

Published by Manish Jain for BPB Publications, 20, Ansari Road, Darya Ganj, New Delhi-110002 and Printed by Repro India Ltd., Mumbai

'C' Programming

'C' is a general-purpose, powerful computer programming language, supporting structured programming and top-down approach.

It was developed by Dennis Ritchie in 1972 at AT & T Bell Labs. It is used to re-implement the Unix operating system.

It is used to design system software such as operating system and compiler, network devices, and develop application software such as database and spreadsheets. A Unix kernel is completely developed in C language.

The best way we learn anything is by practice and exercise questions. Here are some exercise questions with solutions, specially designed for students' practice.

Hope, these exercises will help you to improve your coding skills.

All the best!

Preface

C Question Bank with Solution helps you to understand programming and coding with many questions.

This Book Covers all questions that are deemed important for the interview and examination point of you.

Although care has been taken for accuracy, the possibility of minor inaccuracies cannot be ruled out. Lastly, thank you to all students who believe in me.

Table of Contents

1. How to give output?

The *printf()* function, an inbuilt library function in C, is available in C library by default. The function is declared and the related macros are defined in *stdio.h*, a header file in C.

We have to include the *stdio.h* file while using the *printf()* library function in C language.

In C, the *printf()* function is used to print the character, string, float, integer, octal and hexadecimal values onto the output screen.

The syntax of the *printf()* function is:

printf("Text");
printf("Format string", variable)

1. Write a program to print message:

Welcome students, we are trying to learn C

```
#include <stdio.h>
int main()
 {
   printf("Welcome students,);
   printf("We are trying to learn C");
   return(0);
 }
```

2. Write a program to print your name and phone number:

```
Name:  XXX
Phone:  99-999-99999
#include <stdio.h>
 int main()
  {
    printf("Name:\t XXX\n");
    printf("Phone:\t 99-999-99999\n");
    return(0);

  }
```

3. Write a program to print the first letter of your name, for example, F:

```
#include <stdio.h>
int main()
{
        printf("******\n");
        printf("*\n");
        printf("*\n");
        printf("******\n");
        printf("*\n");
        printf("*\n");
        printf("*\n");

        return(0);
}
```

4. Write a program to print following:

Name	: XXX
DOB	: 1\10\2000
Course	: "C"
Institute	: 'Swati Computers'

```
#include <stdio.h>
int main()
{
        printf("Name\t\t:XXX\n");
        printf("DOB\t\t:1\\10\\2000\n");
        printf("Course\t\t:\"C\"\n");
        printf("Institute\t:\'Swati Computers\'\n");

        return(0);
}
```

5. Write a C program to declare two integer and one float variables, then initialize them to 23, 56, and 34.6. It then prints these values .

```
#include <stdio.h>

int main()
{
    int x;
    int y;
    float z;
```

```
        x=23;
        y=56;
        z=34.6;

        printf("x= %d\n",x);
        printf("y=%d\n",y);
        printf("z=%3.1f\n",z);
        return 0;
}
```

6. Write a program to declare a char variable then initialize it with *, then print A.

```
        #include <stdio.h>
        int main()


        {
        char g='*';
                printf("%10c",g");
                printf("\n%8c %3c",g,g);
                printf("\n%8c %1c %c",g,g,g);
                printf("\n%8c %3c",g,g);

                return(0);
        }
```

7. Write a program to compute the area of a rectangle with height 4 inch and width 8 inch.

```
        #include <stdio.h>

        int main() {
        int width;
        int height;

        int area;

                height = 4;
                width = 8;
                area = height * width;
                printf("\nArea of the rectangle = %d square inches ", area);

        return(0);
        }
```

2. Basic input and output

The *scanf()* function allows you to accept input from standard input, that is, the keyboard.

The syntax for *scanf()* is:

scanf("format string", & variable);

Format specifier	Description
%d	Integer format specifier
%f	Float format specifier
%c	Character format specifier
%s	String format specifier
%u	Unsigned integer format specifier
%ld	Long int format specifier

8. Write a program to compute the area and circumference of a circle with a radius 4 inch.

```
#include <stdio.h>
int main() {
   int radius;
   float area, circ;
   radius = 6;

   circ = 2*3.14*radius;
   printf("Circumference of the Circle = %f inches\n", circ);

      area = 3.14*radius*radius;
   printf("Area of the Circle = %f square inches\n", area);

   return(0);
      }
```

9. Write a program to prompt the user to input their age and print.

```
#include <stdio.h>

int main()
{
   int age;
```

```
        printf("Enter your age:");
        scanf("%d",&age);
        printf("You are %2d years old",age);
        return 0;
}
```

10. Write a program to prompt the user to input two numbers and calculate their addition, subtraction, multiplication, and division.

```
#include <stdio.h>
int main()
{
    int n1,n2,ad,sub,multi,divi;

    printf("Enter 2 numbers:");
    scanf("%d%d",&n1,n2);

        ad=n1+n2;
sub=n1–n2;
multi=n1*n2;
divi=n1/n2;

    printf("\nAddition=%d\nSubtraction=%d",ad,sub);
    printf("\nMultiplication=%d\nDivision=%d",multi,divi);
    return 0;
}
```

11. Write a program to input marks of three subjects and calculate the total and percentage.

```
#include <stdio.h>
int main() {
int eng,maths,science;
float total, percentage;

printf("Enter marks of English, math, science, maximum 100 in each\n");
scanf("%d%d%d",&eng,&math,&science);

total=eng+math +science;

percentage=total/300*100;

printf("\nTotal marks obtained=%d",total);
```

```
printf("\nPercentage scored =%f",percentage);
return(0);
    }
```

12. Write a program to convert specified days into years, weeks, and days (ignore leap year).

```
#include <stdio.h>
int main()
{
    int days, years, weeks;

    days = 1329;

    // Converts days to years, weeks and days
    years = days/365;
    weeks = (days % 365)/7;
    days = days–((years*365) + (weeks*7));

    printf("Years: %d\n", years);
    printf("Weeks: %d\n", weeks);
    printf("Days: %d \n", days);

    return 0;
}
```

13. Write a program to convert a given integer (in seconds) into hours, minutes, and seconds.

```
#include <stdio.h>
int main() {
        int sec, h, m, s;
        printf("Input seconds: ");
        scanf("%d", &sec);

        h = (sec/3600);

        m = (sec – (3600*h))/60;
        s = (sec – (3600*h)–(m*60));

        printf("H:M:S –%d:%d:%d\n",h,m,s);

        return 0;
}
```

14. Write a program to calculate the speed of bike, when the distance and time are given by the user.

```c
#include <stdio.h>
int main() {
        float distance,time,speed;
        printf("Input distance and time taken to travel");
        scanf("%f%f", &distance,&time);
        speed=distance/time;

        printf("\nSpeed calculated : %f",speed);

        return 0;

}
```

15. Write a program that converts a temperature from Centigrade into Fahrenheit.

```c
#include <stdio.h>

int main() {
float temp_f;    /* degrees fahrenheit */
float temp_c;    /* degrees centigrade */

        printf("Input a temperature (in Centigrade): ");
        scanf("%f", &temp_c);

        temp_f = ((9.0 / 5.0) * temp_c) + 32.0;
        printf("\n%f degrees Fahrenheit.\n", temp_f);

        return(0);
}
```

16. Write a program that converts kilometers per hour into miles per hour.

```c
#include <stdio.h>
int main()
{
float kmph;              /* kilometers per hour */
float miph;              /* miles per hour (to be computed) */
        printf("Input kilometers per hour: ");
                scanf("%f", &kmph);

        miph = (kmph * 0.6213712);
        printf("\n%f miles per hour\n", miph);

        return(0);

}
```

17. Write a program to input two numbers and interchange their values without using any third variable.

```
#include <stdio.h>
int main()
{
int a,b;
printf("enter 2 numbers");
scanf("%d%d",&a,&b);

a=a+b;
b=a-b;
a=a-b;
Printf("\nAfter Swaping a=%d and b=%d",a,b);

return(0);}
```

18. Write a program to calculate simple interest when P, R, and T are given by the user.

```
#include <stdio.h>

int main()
{
    float principle, time, rate, SI;

        /* Input principle, rate and time */
    printf("Enter principle (amount): ");
    scanf("%f", &principle);

    printf("Enter time: ");
    scanf("%f", &time);

    printf("Enter rate: ");
    scanf("%f", &rate);

    SI = (principle * time * rate) / 100;
    printf("Simple Interest = %f", SI);

    return 0;
}
```

19. Write a program in C to calculate the sum of three numbers to obtain input in one line separated by a comma.

```
#include<stdio.h>
int main()
{
int num1,num2,num3;        /* declaration of three variables */
int sum;
char line_text[50];        /* line of input from keyboard */

    printf("Input three numbers separated by comma : ");

    fgets(line_text, sizeof(line_text), stdin);

    sscanf(line_text, "%d, %d, %d", &num1, &num2,
    &num3);

sum = num1+num2+num3;
printf("\nThe sum of three numbers : %d\n", sum);

    return(0);
}
```

20. Write a program to input the quantity of pens and price of each pen purchased, and calculate the total amount payable.

```
#include<stdio.h>
int main()
{
int qty_pen;
float amt,price_pen;

    printf("Enter quantity and of pen and price of 1 pen : ");
        scanf("%d%f",&qty_pen,&price_pen);

amt=qty_pen * price_pen;
    printf("\nAmount Payable=%f",amt);
    return(0);
}
```

21. Write a program to calculate the total salary when the basic salary is given by the user and calculate HRA, DA, and TA.

```
#include<stdio.h>
int main()
{
float total,Basic,HRA,TA,DA;
    printf("Enter basic salary : ");
        scanf ("%f",&Basic);

HRA=Basic *10/100;
TA= Basic *8/100;
DA=Basic * 5/100;

Total= Basic +HRA +DA +TA;
    printf("\nTotal Salary = %f",total);
    return(0);
}
```

22. Write a program to calculate the amount payable after 10% discount on purchase in a sale.

```
#include<stdio.h>
int main()
{
float amt, PR, dis;
    printf("Enter Purchase Rate : ");
        scanf ("%f",&PR);

dis=PR*10/100;
amt=PR–dis;

    printf("\nAmount Payable = %f",amt);
    return(0);
}
```

3. Using the ternary statement

Using *?:* reduces the number of lines of codes and improves the performance of an application.

Its syntax is as follows:

expression-1 ? expression-2 : expression-3

In the afore mentioned syntax, *expression-1* is the condition, and *expression-2* and *expression-3* will be either a value or variable or statement or any mathematical expression.

If the condition is true, *expression-2* is executed; otherwise, *expression-3* is executed.

23. Write a program using the ternary operator to check whether a given number is even or odd.

```
#include<stdio.h>
int main()
{
int n;
    printf("Enter  a number : ");
        scan(" %d",&n);

(n%2==0)? Printf("\nnumber is even") : printf("\nNumber is
odd");
    return(0);
}
```

24. Write a program using the ternary operator to check whether a given number is positive or negative.

```
#include<stdio.h>
int main()
{
int n;
    printf("Enter  a number : ");
        scan(" %d",&n);

(n>0)? printf("\nnumber is positive") : printf("\nNumber is
Negative");
    return(0);
}
```

25. Write a program using the ternary operator to return greater number out of two numbers.

```
#include<stdio.h>
int main()
{
int a,b,x;
    printf("Enter  two numbers : ");
        scan(" %d%d",&a,&b);

x=(a>b) ? a : b;
        Printf("\nGreater is %d",x);
    return(0);
}
```

26. Write a program using the ternary operator to check whether the gender is male or female.

```
#include<stdio.h>
int main()
{
char g;
    printf("Enter Gender M/F : ");
        scan(" %c",&g);

(g=='M')? printf("\nHello Sir") : printf("\nHello mam");
    return(0);
}
```

27. Write a program to check gender is Male/ female use OR operator, using Ternary operator.

```
#include<stdio.h>
int main()
{
char g;
    printf("Enter Gender M/F : ");
        scan(" %c",&g);

(g=='M' || g=='m')? printf("\nHello Sir") : printf("\nHello
mam");
    return(0);
}
```

28. Write a program using the OR operator and ternary operator to check whether the gender is male or female.

```
#include<stdio.h>
int main()
{
char g;
    printf("Enter Gender M/F : ");
        scan(" %c",&g);

(g=='M' || g=='m')? printf("\nHello Sir") : (g=='F' ||
g=='f')?printf("\nHello mam");
    return(0);
}
```

29. Write a program to find the greatest number out of three numbers, using the ternary operator.

```
#include<stdio.h>
int main()
{
int a,b,c;
        printf("enter 3 numbers");
        scanf("%d%d%d",&a,&b,&c);

(a>b)?(a>c)?printf("A is greater"): printf("\nC is
greater"):(b>c)?printf("\nB is greater"):printf("\nC is greater");

    return(0);
}
```

30. Write a program to check whether a person is eligible to vote or not, using the ternary operator (eligibility criterion: age should be more than 18 years).

```
#include<stdio.h>
int main()
{
int age;
    printf("Enter your age ");
        scan(" %d",&age);

(age>=18) ? printf("\nEligible ") : printf("\nNot Eligible");
    return(0);
}
```

4. Decision-making practice: if-else and switch case

Decision-making is used to specify the order of execution of the statements.

An *if* statement can be followed by an optional *else* statement, which executes when the Boolean expression is false.

The C programming language assumes any non-zero and non-null values as true, and if it is either zero or null, then it is assumed as a false value.

The syntax of an if-else statement is:

```
if(Condition)
{
Statements, if condition is true
    }
    Else
    {
    Statements, if condition is false
        }
```

An if statement can be followed by an optional else if...else statement, which is very useful to test various conditions using a single if...else if statement.

A*s witch* statement allows a variable to be tested for equality against a list of values.

A switch statement can be replaced by an if-else statement.

Its syntax is:

```
switch(expression) {
  case constant-expression  :
     statement(s);
     break; /* optional */

          case constant-expression  :

     statement(s);
     break; /* optional */

     /* you can have any number of case statements */
     default : /* Optional */
     statement(s);
  }
```

31. Write a program to check whether a character is a vowel or consonant.

```c
#include<stdio.h>
int main()
{
char v;
    printf("Enter a character ");
            scan(" %c",&v);
if(v=='a' || v=='e' || v=='i' || v=='o' || v=='u')
    {
            printf("\nvowel");
    }
else
    {
            printf("\nConsonent");
    }

    return(0);
}
```

32. Write a program to find the tallest person between two persons.

```c
#include<stdio.h>
int main()
{
int a,b,x;
    printf("Enter  height of 2 persons : ");
            scan(" %d%d",&a,&b);

if(a>b)
    {
            Printf("a is greater");
    }
else
    {
            Printf("b is greater");
    }
    return(0);
}
```

33. Write a program to accept two integers and check whether they are equal or not.

```
#include <stdio.h>
void main()
{
    int int1, int2;

    printf("Input the values for Number1 and Number2 : ");
    scanf("%d %d", &int1, &int2);

    if (int1 == int2)
        printf("Number1 and Number2 are equal\n");
    else
        printf("Number1 and Number2 are not equal\n");
}
```

34. Write a program to find whether a given year is a leap year or not.

```
#include <stdio.h>
void main()
{
    int chk_year;

    printf("Input a year :");
    scanf("%d", &chk_year);

    if ((chk_year % 400) == 0)
        printf("%d is a leap year.\n", chk_year);
    else if ((chk_year % 100) == 0)
        printf("%d is a not leap year.\n", chk_year);
    else if ((chk_year % 4) == 0)
        printf("%d is a leap year.\n", chk_year);
    else
        printf("%d is not a leap year \n", chk_year);
}
```

35. Write a program to change the case of an input char. If it is in capital (upper case), then convert into lower case and vice versa.

```
#include<stdio.h>
int main()
```

```
{
char ch;
    printf("Enter a character : ");
            scan(" %c",&ch);

if(ch>=65 && ch<=90)
{
            ch=ch+32;
}
Else
{
            ch=ch–32
}
    return(0);
}
```

36. Write a program to check the greatest number out of three given numbers.

```
#include<stdio.h>
int main()
{
int a,b,c;
        printf("enter 3 numbers");
        scanf("%d%d%d",&a,&b,&c);

if(a>b)
{
        If(a>c)
        {
                printf("a is greater");
}
else
{
        printf("c is greater");
}
}
else if(b>c)
{
        printf("b is greater");
}
else
{
```

```
        printf("c is greater");
}
    return(0);
}
```

37. Write a program to check the greater number out of three given numbers.

```
#include<stdio.h>
int main()
{
int a,b,c;
        printf("enter 3 numbers");
        scanf("%d%d%d",&a,&b,&c);

if(a>b && a>c)
{
        printf("\n a is greater");
}
else if(b>a && b>c)
{
        printf("\b b is greater");
}
else if(c>a && c>b)
{
        printf("\n c is greater");
}
    return(0);
}
```

38. Write a program to input a grade and display the description.

```
#include <stdio.h>

void main()
{
    char grd;

    printf("Input the grade :");
    scanf("%c", &grd);

    switch(grd)
    {
    case 'E':
```

```
printf( " Excellent");
    break;
  case 'V':
printf( " Very Good");
    break;
  case 'G':
printf( " Good ");
    break;
  case 'A':
printf( " Average");
    break;
  case 'F':
printf( " Fails");
    break;
  default :
printf( "Invalid Grade Found. \n");
    break;
  }
}
```

39. Write a program to read any day in integer and display the day name in words.

```
#include <stdio.h>
void main()
{
  int dayno;
  printf("Input Day No : ");
  scanf("%d",&dayno);

  switch(dayno)
  {
      case 1:
          printf("Monday \n");
          break;
      case 2:
          printf("Tuesday \n");
          break;
      case 3:
          printf("Wednesday \n");
          break;
      case 4:
```

```
            printf("Thursday \n");
            break;
        case 5:
            printf("Friday \n");
            break;
        case 6:
            printf("Saturday \n");
            break;
        case 7:
            printf("Sunday \n");
            break;
        default:
            printf("Invalid day number. \nPlease try again
....\n");
            break;
    }
}
```

40. Write a program to read any month number in integer and display the number of days for this month.

```
#include <stdio.h>
void main()
{
  int monno;

  printf("Input Month No : ");
  scanf("%d",&monno);

  switch(monno)
  {
        case 1:
        case 3:
        case 5:
        case 7:
        case 8:
        case 10:
        case 12:
            printf("Month have 31 days. \n");
            break;
        case 2:
            printf("The 2nd month is a February and have 28
```

days. \n");

     printf("in leap year The February month Have 29

days.\n");

    break;

   case 4:

   case 6:

   case 9:

   case 11:

    printf("Month have 30 days. \n");

    break;

default:

    printf("invalid Month number.\nPlease try again

....\n");

    break;

  }

}

41. Write a menu-driven program to perform a simple calculation.

```
#include <stdio.h>
void main() {
  int num1,num2,opt;

  printf("Enter the first Integer :");
  scanf("%d",&num1);

  printf("Enter the second Integer :");
  scanf("%d",&num2);

  printf("\nInput your option :\n");
  printf("1-Addition.\n2-Subtraction.\n3-Multiplication.\n4-
  Division.\n5-Exit.\n");
   scanf("%d",&opt);

   switch(opt) {
    case 1:
      printf("The Addition of  %d and %d is:
      %d\n",num1,num2,num1+num2);
      break;

    case 2:
      printf("The Subtraction of %d  and %d is:
      %d\n",num1,num2,num1–num2);
      break;
```

```
        case 3:
         printf("The Multiplication of %d  and %d is:
         %d\n",num1,num2,num1*num2);
         break;

        case 4:
         if(num2==0) {
          printf("The second integer is zero. Divide by zero.\n");
         } else {
          printf("The Division of %d  and %d is :
          %d\n",num1,num2,num1/num2);
         }
         break;

        case 5:
         break;

        default:
         printf("Input correct option\n");
         break;
       }
      }
```

42. Write a program to calculate the electricity bill of a given customer. The unit consumed by the user should be taken from the keyboard, and display the total amount to be paid by the customer. The charges are as follows:

Unit	Charge/unit
Upto 199	@1.20
200 and above, but less than 400	@1.50
400 and above, but less than 600	@1.80
600 and above	@2.00

If the bill exceeds Rs. 400, then a surcharge of 15% will be charged and the minimum bill should be of Rs. 100.

```
#include <stdio.h>
void main()
{
  float chg, surchg=0, gramt,netamt;

  printf("Input the unit consumed by the customer : ");
```

```
scanf("%d",&conu);

if (conu <200 )
        chg = 1.20;
else    if (conu>=200 && conu<400)
                chg = 1.50;
        else if (conu>=400 && conu<600)
                        chg = 1.80;
                else
                        chg = 2.00;
gramt = conu*chg;
if (gramt>300)
        surchg = gramt*15/100.0;
netamt = gramt+surchg;
if (netamt  < 100)
        netamt =100;
printf("\nElectricity Bill\n");
printf("unit Consumed: %d\n",conu);
printf("Amount Charges @Rs. %4.2f  per unit :%8.2f\
n",chg,gramt);
printf("Surchage Amount: %8.2f\n",surchg);
printf("Net Amount Paid By the Customer: %8.2f\
n",netamt);

}
```

43. Write a program to calculate the profit and loss in a transaction.

```
#include <stdio.h>
void main()
{
   int cprice,sprice, plamt;

   printf("Input Cost Price: ");
   scanf("%d", &cprice);

   printf("Input Selling Price: ");
   scanf("%d", &sprice);

   if(sprice>cprice) //calculate profit
   {
      plamt = sprice–cprice;
      printf("\nYou can booked your profit amount : %d\n",
plamt);
   }
```

```
        else if(cprice>sprice) //calculate loss
        {
           plamt = cprice–sprice;
           printf("\nYou got a loss of amount : %d\n", plamt);
        }
        else //No Profit No Loss
        {
           printf("\nYou are running in no profit no loss condition.\n");
        }
    }
```

44. Write a program to input a number and print its ASCII-equivlent value.

```
        #include<stdio.h>
        void main()
        {
        int n;
                printf("enter a number");
                scanf("%d",&n);

        printf("\nascii value for %d is %c",n,n);
        }
```

45. Write a program to calculate the amount payable after deducting the discount on the purchase amount.

Discounts are as follows:

Purchase amount >=8,000; Discount=10% on the purchase amount
Purchase amount >=5,000; Discount =8% on the purchase amount
Purchase amount >=1,000; Discount =4% on the purchase amount
Otherwise; Discount = Rs. 100

```
        #include<stdio.h>
        void main()
        {
        float PR,dis,amount;
                printf("enter purchase rate");
                scanf("%f",&PR);

                If(PR>=8000)
                 dis=PR* .10;
                else if(PR>=5000)
                 dis=PR*.08;
                else if(PR>=1000)
```

```
                Dis=PR*.04;
        else
         dis=100;

        amount=PR–dis;
        printf("\nAmont payable after %f discount  is
        %f",dis,amt);

}
```

46. Write a program to calculate the total salary after giving HRA, DA, and TA with the basic salary.

HRA, DA, and TA should be calculated as follows:
Basic salary > =10,000 HRA=8%, DA=7%, TA= 8%
Basic salary > =5,000   HRA=6%, DA=5%, TA= 7%
Otherwise   HRA=5%, DA=5%, TA= 7%

```
#include<stdio.h>
        void main()
        {
        float  basic_sal, hra,da,ta,total_sal;
                printf("enter basic salary");
                scanf("%f",&basic_sal);

                if(basic_sal >=10000)
                {
                hra=basic_sal*.08;
                da=basic_sal*.07;
                ta=basic_sal*.08;
}
else if(basic_sal >=5000)
                {
                hra=basic_sal*.06;
                da=basic_sal*.05;
                ta=basic_sal*.07;
}
else
{
hra=basic_sal*.05;
                da=basic_sal*.05;
                ta=basic_sal*.07;
}
total_sal=basic_sal+hra+da+ta;
printf("\nbasic salary=%f \nhra=%f \t da=%f \t ta=%f",basic_
sal,hra,da,ta);
```

```
printf("\ntotal salary=%f",total_sal);
}
```

47. Write a program to output a message according to the age and gender.

```
#include<stdio.h>
void main()
{
char gender;
int age;
printf("enter gender m/f");
gender=getchar();

printf("enter age");
scanf("%d",&age);
if(gender=='m' || gender=='m')
{
        if(age>=65)
         printf("hello uncle");
        else if(age>=35)
         printf("hello sir");
        else
         printf("hello young boy");
}
else if(gender=='f' || gender=='F')
        {
        if(age>=70)
         printf("hello aunty");
        else if(age>=25)
         printf("hello mam");
        else
         printf("hello baby");
}

}
```

48. Write a menu-driven program to print a message or star using *goto*.

```
#include<stdio.h>
#include<stdlib.h>
int main()
{
```

```
int n;
        printf("Enter choice to print\npress 1 for print message\
        npress 2 for print star \n stop\n");
        scanf("%d",&n);

        switch(n)
        {
        case 1:
                        goto msg;
        case 2:
                        goto star;
        default:
                        exit(0);
        }
        msg:
                {
                printf("Hello");
                exit(0);
                }
        star:
                {
                printf("\n*");
                exit(0);
                }
}
```

49. Write a program to output one-digit password without showing it at runtime.

```
#include<stdio.h>
#include<conio.h>
void main()
{
char password;
        printf("enter 1 digit password");
        password=getch();
        printf("*");
}
```

5. Looping/Iteration

Loops are used in programming to repeat a specific block of code for multiple (N) times until some end condition is met.
Loops can be categorized into two types:

- Entry control loop
- Exit control loop

Examples of an entry control loop are the for loop and the while loop.
Example of an exit control loop is the do-while loop.
The syntax for the for loop is:
for (variable initialization; condition; variable update)

```
{
   Code to execute while the condition is true
}
```

The syntax for the while loop is
while (condition) { Code to execute while the condition is true

```
}
```

The syntax for the do loop is:
```
do {
       Code to execute
       } while ( condition );
```

More syntaxes that are not error are:
```
           int i;
for(i=1;;i++){ if(condition) break;}
for(;;){} // infinite loop,but no error
for(i=1;i<=10&&i>=3;i++){}
for(i=1;i<=10;i++);
```

```
while(1){} //infinite loop
while(1){ if(condition)break;}
```

Jumping statements

Jumping statements are used to exit loop / continue in loop / go to a particular position.

Types of jump statements are:
- Break
- Continue

- Goto
- Return

Break

The *break* statement is used inside a loop or a switch statement.
When a compiler finds the break statement inside a loop, it will abort the loop and continue to execute statements followed by the loop.

A *break* statement is used to terminate the execution of the rest of the block where it is present and takes the control out of the block to the next statement.
The syntax of the break statement is:

for(;;){ if (condition){break;}}

Continue

Continue is another keyword that controls the flow of loops. If you are executing a loop and hit a continue statement, the loop will stop its current iteration, update itself (in the case of for loops), and begin to execute again from the top.

Continue is mostly used in loops. Rather than terminating the loop, it stops the execution of the statements underneath and takes control of the next iteration.

The *continue* statement passes the control to the next iteration of the inner loop where it is present and not to any of the outer loops.
The syntax of a continue statement is:

for(;;){if(condition){continue;}}

Goto

The *goto* jump statement is used to transfer the flow of control to any desired part of the program.
It jumps from one point to another point within a function.

The syntax of a goto statement is:

goto label;

Note: Use of a goto statement is highly discouraged in any programming language because it makes it difficult to trace the control flow of a program, making the program difficult to understand and modify.
Any program that uses a goto statement can be rewritten to avoid it.

Return

The *return* statement is used to terminate the execution of a function and transfer the program control back to the calling function.

The return statement ends the current function and returns control to the point of invocation. It can also return a value in that point.

A function may or may not return a value.
A return statement returns a value to the calling function and assigns to the variable on the left side of the calling function.

If a function does not return a value, the return type in the function definition and declaration is specified as void.

The syntax of a return statement is:
return expr ;
where *expr* is the expression whose value is returned by the function.
The execution of the return statement causes the expression *expr* to be to be evaluated and its value to be returned to the point from which this function is called.
The expression *expr* in the return statement is optional, and if omitted, the program control is transferred back to the calling function, without returning any value.

50. Write a program to print the seriers 1 to N using the for loop.

```
#include<stdio.h>
void main()
{
int i,n;
        printf("enter value of n");
        scanf("%d",&n);

        for(i=1;i<=n;i++)
        {
        printf("\n%d",i);
}
}
```

51. Write a program to print the square seriers 1 to N using the for loop.

```
#include<stdio.h>
void main()
{
int i,n;
```

```
                printf("enter value of n");
                scanf("%d",&n);

                for(i=1;i<=n;i++)
                {
                printf("\n%d",i*i);
        }
        }
```

52. Write a program to print the cube seriers 1 to N using the for loop.

```
        #include<stdio.h>
        void main()
        {
        int i,n;
                printf("enter value of n");
                scanf("%d",&n);

                for(i=1;i<=n;i++)
                {
                printf("\n%d",i*i*i);
        }
        }
```

53. Write a program to print the seriers 1 to N, its square, and cube using the for loop.

```
        #include<stdio.h>
        void main()
        {
        int i,n;
                printf("enter value of n");
                scanf("%d",&n);

                for(i=1;i<=n;i++)
                {
                printf("\n%d\t%d\t%d",i,i*i,i*i*i);
        }
        }
```

54. Write a program to find the even/odd number between 1 to N using the for loop.

```c
#include<stdio.h>
void main()
{
int i,n;
        printf("enter value of n");
        scanf("%d",&n);

        for(i=1;i<=n;i++)
        {
        If(i %2 ==0)
        {
                Printf("\n%d is even",i);
}
        Else
        {

                Printf("\n%d is odd",i);

        }
        }
        }
```

55. Write a program to print a table of the given number.

```c
#include<stdio.h>
void main()
{
int i,n;
        printf("enter number");
        scanf("%d",&n);

        for(i=1;i<=10;i++)
        {
        printf("\n%d*%d=%d",n,i,n*i);
        }
        }
```

56. Write a program to print the seriers 1,3,5,7,9 ....N using the for loop.

```
#include<stdio.h>
void main()
{
int i,n;
        printf("enter value of n");
        scanf("%d",&n);

        for(i=1;i<=n*2;i+=2)
        {
        printf("\n%d",i);
}
}
```

57. Write a program to print the seriers 2,4,6,8...N using the for loop.

```
#include<stdio.h>
void main()
{
int i,n;
        printf("enter value of n");
        scanf("%d",&n);

        for(i=2;i<=n*2;i+=2)
        {
        printf("\n%d",i);
}
}
```

58. Write a program to print the seriers 1,5,2,10,3,15....N using the for loop.

```
#include<stdio.h>
void main()
{
int i,n;
        printf("enter value of n");
        scanf("%d",&n);

        for(i=1;i<=n;i++)
        {
        printf("%d,%d,",i,i*5);
}
Printf("\b ");
}
```

59. Write a program to print the seriers 1,0,1,0,1,0,1,....N using the for loop.

```
#include<stdio.h>
void main()
{
int i,n,x=1;
        printf("enter value of n");
        scanf("%d",&n);

        for(i=1;i<=n;i++)
        {
        printf("%d,",x);
        x=1-x;
}
Printf("\b ");
}
Or
#include<stdio.h>
void main()
{
int i,n,x=1;
        printf("enter value of n");
        scanf("%d",&n);

        for(i=1;i<=n;i++)
        {
                if(i%2==0)
                printf("1,");
                else
                printf("0,");
}
printf("\b ");
}
```

60. Write a program to print the seriers 1,–1,1,–1,1,–1,....N using the for loop.

```
#include<stdio.h>
void main()
{
int i,n,x=1;
        printf("enter value of n");
        scanf("%d",&n);

        for(i=1;i<=n;i++)
```

```
        {
        printf("%d,",x);
        x=x * (–1);
}
Printf("\b ");
}
Or
#include<stdio.h>
void main()
{
int i,n,x=1;
        printf("enter value of n");
        scanf("%d",&n);

        for(i=1;i<=n;i++)
        {
                if(i%2==0)
                printf("1,");
                else
                printf("–1,");
}
printf("\b ");
}
```

61. Write a program to read 10 numbers from keyboard and find their sum and average.

```
#include <stdio.h>
void main()
{
   int i,n,sum=0;
        float avg;
        printf("Input the 10 numbers : \n");
        for (i=1;i<=10;i++)
        {
          printf("Number–%d :",i);

                scanf("%d",&n);
                sum +=n;
        }
        avg=sum/10.0;
        printf("The sum of 10 no is : %d\nThe Average is :
%f\n",sum,avg);
}
```

62. Write a program to find the lowest common multiple (LCM) of any two numbers.

```
#include <stdio.h>

void main()
{
    int i, n1, n2, max, lcm=1;

    printf("\n\n  LCM of two numbers:\n ");
    printf("---------------------\n");

    printf("Input 1st number for LCM: ");
    scanf("%d", &n1);
    printf("Input 2nd number for LCM: ");
    scanf("%d", &n2);

    max = (n1>n2) ? n1 : n2;

    for(i=max;  ; i+=max)
    {

        if(i%n1==0 && i%n2==0)
        {
            lcm = i;
            break;
        }
    }

    printf("\nLCM of %d and %d = %d\n\n", n1, n2, lcm);

}
```

63. Write a program to find the HCF (highest common factor) of two numbers.

```
#include <stdio.h>

void main()
{
    int i, n1, n2, j, hcf=1;

    printf("\n\n  HCF of two numbers:\n ");
    printf("---------------------\n");

    printf("Input 1st number for HCF: ");
    scanf("%d", &n1);
    printf("Input 2nd number for HCF: ");
    scanf("%d", &n2);
```

```
        j = (n1<n2) ? n1 : n2;
        for(i=1; i<=j; i++)
        {
            if(n1%i==0 && n2%i==0)
            {
                hcf = i;
            }
        }
        printf("\nHCF of %d and %d is : %d\n\n", n1, n2, hcf);
}
```

64. Write a program to find the factorial of a given number using the while loop.

```
#include<stdio.h>
void main()
{
int n,f=1;
        printf("enter value of n");
        scanf("%d",&n);

        while(n>=1)
{
f=f*n;
n=n-1;
}
printf("\nfactorial=%d",f);
}
```

65. Write a program to find the factorial of a given number using the for loop.

```
#include<stdio.h>
void main()
{
int n,f=1,i;
        printf("enter value of n");
        scanf("%d",&n);

        for(i=1;i<=n;i++)
{
        f=f*i;
}
printf("\nfactorial=%d",f);
}
```

66. Write a program to input numbers until the user enters 99.

```
#include<stdio.h>
void main()
{
int n,f=1;
        printf("enter value of n");
        scanf("%d",&n);

        while(n!=99)
{
printf("enter another number");
        scanf("%d",&n);
}
printf("\Thanks for using program..);
}
```

67. Write a program to convert a binary number into a decimal number using the math function.

```
#include <stdio.h>
#include <math.h>
void main()
{       int n1, n;
        int dec=0,i=0,j,d;

        printf("Input the binary number :");
        scanf("%d",&n);

        n1=n;

        while(n!=0)
        {
d = n % 10;
                dec=dec+d*pow(2,i);
                n=n/10;
                i++;
        }

        printf("\nThe Binary Number : %d\nThe equivalent
        Decimal Number is : %d\n\n",n1,dec);

}
```

68. Write a program in C to find the sum of GP series.

```c
#include <stdio.h>
#include <math.h>

void main()
{

    float g1,cr,i,n,j;
    float ntrm,gpn;
    float sum=0;

    printf("Input the first number of the G.P. series: ");
    scanf("%f",&g1);

    printf("Input the number or terms in the G.P. series: ");
    scanf("%f",&ntrm);

    printf("Input the common ratio of G.P. series: ");
    scanf("%f",&cr);

    printf("\nThe numbers for the G.P. series:\n ");
        printf("%f ",g1);

        sum=g1;

    for(j=1;j<ntrm;j++)
      {
      gpn=g1*pow(cr,j);
                sum=sum+gpn;
      printf("%f ",gpn);
      }

    printf("\nThe Sum of the G.P. series : %f\n\n",sum);
}
```

69. Write a program to input the four-digit ATM pin. (pin should not be visible).

```c
#include<stdio.h>
void main()
{
char pin;
int i;
        for(i=1;i<=4;i++)
        {
        pin=getch();
        printf("*");
```

```
        }
    printf("\nThanks for Entering");
    }
```

70. Write a program to calculate X=NP.

```
#include<stdio.h>
void main()
{
int n,p,x=1;

printf("enter number and power");
scanf("%d%d",&n,&p);

while(p>=1)
{
        x=x*n;
        p--;
}
printf("\ncalculation=%d",x);
}
```

6. Use of Goto

71. Write a menu-driven program for +, –, and * without using any loop.

```c
#include<stdio.h>
#include<stdlib.h>
void main()
{
int num1,num2,ans,choice;

start:{

printf("\nenter choice:\npress 1 for addition\npress 2 for subtract\npress 3 for multliplication\npress any other for exit\n");
scanf("%d",&choice);

if(choice==1)
 goto addi;
else if(choice==2)
 goto subt;
else if(choice==3)
 goto multi;
else
        goto stop;
}

addi:{
printf("\nenter 2 numbers");
scanf("%d%d",&num1,&num2);
ans=num1+num2;
printf("\naddition of %d and %d is %d",num1,num2,ans);
goto start;
}

subt:{
printf("\nenter 2 numbers");
scanf("%d%d",&num1,&num2);
ans=num1-num2;
printf("\nsubtraction of %d and %d is %d",num1,num2,ans);
goto start;

}

multi:{
printf("\nenter 2 numbers");
```

```
scanf("%d%d",&num1,&num2);
ans=num1*num2;
printf("\nmultiplication of %d and %d is %d",num1,num2,ans);
goto start;

}
stop:{
        exit(0);
}

}
```

72. Write a program to print the Fibonacci series 0,1,1,2,3,5,8...N.

```
#include<stdio.h>
void main()
{
int i=0,j=1,n;
        printf("enter value of n");
        scanf("%d",&n);

        while(i<=n)
        {
        printf("\n%d",i);
        j=i+j;
i=j–i;
}
}
```

73. Write a program to print a number in the reverse order.
    Example: Input N=123; output 321

```
            #include<stdio.h>
void main()
{
int num,rev=0,remainder;
        printf("enter number");
        scanf("%d",&num);

        while(num!=0)
        {
        remainder=num%10;
        rev=rev*10+remainder;
num=num/10;
}
printf("\nreverse number=%d",rev);
```

```
}
```

74. Write a program to check whether a given number is palindrome or not.

```
#include<stdio.h>
void main()
{
int num,rev=0,remainder,X;
        printf("enter number");
        scanf("%d",&num);
                X=num;
        while(num!=0)
        {
        remainder=num%10;
        rev=rev*10+remainder;
num=num/10;
}
If(rev==X)
printf("\nNumber is palindrome");
else
printf("\nNot Palindrome");
        }
```

75. Write a program to check whether a given number is Armstrong or not.
Example: N=153 ; (1*1*1) + (5*5*5) + (3*3*3)=153

```
#include<stdio.h>
void main()
{
int num,rev=0,remainder,X;
        printf("enter number");
        scanf("%d",&num);
                X=num;
        while(num!=0)
        {
        remainder=num%10;
        rev=rev+(remainder * remainder * remainder);
num=num/10;
}
If(rev==X)
printf("\nNumber is Armstrong");
else
printf("\nNot Armstrong");
        }
```

76. Write a program to print the sum of each digit of given number.

```
#include<stdio.h>
void main()
{
int num,rev=0,remainder,sum=0;
        printf("enter number");
        scanf("%d",&num);

        while(num!=0)
        {
        remainder=num%10;
        sum=sum+remainder
num=num/10;
}
printf("\nSum of each digits is %d",sum);
        }
```

77. Write a program to print the table of each digit of given number.

```
#include<stdio.h>
void main()
{
int num,rev=0,remainder,i;
        printf("enter number");
        scanf("%d",&num);

        while(num!=0)
        {
        remainder=num%10;
                        for(i=1;i<=10;i++)
                        {
                                printf("%d * %d=
%d",remainder,i,remainder*i);
                        }
        num=num/10;
        printf("\n\n");
}
        }
```

78. Write a program to check whether two given numbers are amicable are not.

Hint: Proper divisior of the first number = second number, and proper divisor of the second number= first number.

```c
#include<stdio.h>
void main()
{
int num1,num2,i,r,sum1=0,sum2=0
printf("enter num1");
scanf("\n%d",&num1);
printf("enter num2");
scanf("\n%d",&num2);
        for(i=1;i<=num1/2;i++)
            {
                if(num1%i==0)

                sum1=sum1+i;
            }
                for(i=1;i<=num2/2;i++)
            {
                if(num2%i==0)
                sum2=sum2+i;
            }
                if(num1==sum2 && num2==sum1)
        printf("\nnumber is amicable");
                else
        printf("\nnot a amicable number");*/

}
```

79. Find the factorial of given number using the do-while loop.

```c
#include<stdio.h>
void main()
{
int f=1,n;
        printf("enter number");
        scanf("%d",&n);

        do{
        f=f*n;
        n--;
        }
```

```
                while(n>=1);

                printf("\nfactorial=%d",f);
        }
```

80. Write a program to display the *n* terms of harmonic series and their sum.

    The series is : 1 + 1/2 + 1/3 + 1/4 + 1/5 ... 1/n

    ```
    #include <stdio.h>
    void main()
    {
      int i,n;
      float s=0.0;
      printf("Input the number of terms : ");
      scanf("%d",&n);
      printf("\n\n");
      for(i=1;i<=n;i++)
      {
         if(i<n)
         {
         printf("1/%d + ",i);
         s+=1/(float)i;
         }
         if(i==n)
         {
         printf("1/%d ",i);
         s+=1/(float)i;
         }
         }
             printf("\nSum of Series upto %d terms : %f \n",n,s);
      }
    ```

81. Write a program to check whether a given number is a perfect number or not.

    ```
    #include <stdio.h>

    void main()
    {
      int n,i,sum;
      int mn,mx;

      printf("Input the number : ");
      scanf("%d",&n);
       sum = 0;
    ```

```
        printf("The positive divisor : ");
        for (i=1;i<n;i++)
        {
        if(n%i==0)
            {
            sum=sum+i;
            printf("%d ",i);
            }
        }
    printf("\nThe sum of the divisor is : %d",sum);
        if(sum==n)
            printf("\nSo, the number is perfect.");
        else
            printf("\nSo, the number is not perfect.");
    printf("\n");
    }
```

82. Write a program to determine whether a given number is prime or not.

```
        #include <stdio.h>
        void main(){

            int num,i,temp=0;

            printf("Input  a number: ");
            scanf("%d",&num);

            for(i=2;i<=num/2;i++){
                if(num % i==0){
        temp=1;
                break;
            }
        }

        if(temp==0)
            printf("%d is a prime number.\n",num);
        else
            printf("%d is not a prime number",num);
        }
```

83. Write a program to convert a decimal number into binary.

```
#include <stdio.h>

void main()
    {
    int n, i, j, binno=0,decimal_num;

    printf("Enter a number to convert : ");
    scanf("%d",&n);

    decimal_num =n;
    i=1;

     for(j=n;j>0;j=j/2)
       {
       binno=binno+(n%2)*i;
       i=i*10;
       n=n/2;
       }
        printf("\nThe Binary of %d is %d.\n\n", decimal_num,binno);
    }
```

84. Write a program to implement all operations of an ATM.

```
#include <stdio.h>
#include <conio.h>
#include<stdlib.h>
int main()
        {
int a=5000,ch=1,d,i;
char pin;

        printf("\n please enter your 4 digit secret ATM pin:\n");
        for(i=1;i<=4;i++)
          {
        pin=getch();
        printf("*");
        if(pin!='0')
           {
                printf("Invalid Pin,Try again");
                return 0;
           }
          }
          }

        while(ch!=4)
```

```
{
printf("\n please enter your choice:\n");
printf("1.enter 1 to check you balance \n");
printf("2.enter 2 for deposit \n");
printf("\n3.enter 3 for withdrawal\n");
printf("\n4. enter 4 for exit.");
scanf("%d",&ch);
switch(ch)
{
case 1:
        printf("\n your balance is %d",a);
        break;
case 2:
        printf("\n please enter amount to deposit");
        scanf("%d",&d);
        a=a+d;
        printf("\n after deposit your balance is %d",a);
        break;
case 3:
        printf("\n please enter amount to withdrawal:");
        scanf("%d",&d);
        if(d%100==0)
        {
        if(d<=a)
        {
        a=a-d;
        printf("\n after withdrawal your amount
        is%d:",a);
        }
        else{ printf("\n u have not suffcient amount in
        your account");
        }
        }
        else
        {
        printf("\n please enter amount of multiple of
        100");
        getch();
        }
        break;
```

```
                case 4:
                        printf("\n thanks for using your ATM, visit us
                        again");

            }
            }

        return 1;
        }
```

85. Write a program to find the smallest of the three numbers.

```
        #include<stdio.h>
        int main()
        {
                int a,b,c;
                        printf("enter 3 no");
                        scanf("%d%d%d",&a,&b,&c);
                        if(a<b)
                        {
                        if(a<c)
                        {
                        printf("%d is smaller",a);
                        }
                        else
                            {
                            printf("%d is smaller",c);
                            }
                        }
                        else if(b<c)
                        {
                        printf("%d is smaller",b);
                        }
                        else
                        {
                        printf("%d is smaller",c);
                        }

        }
```

7. Goto

A goto statement in C programming provides an unconditional jump from the *goto* to a labeled statement in the same function.

The goto statement transfers control to a label. The given label must reside in the same function and can appear before only one statement in the same function.

The syntax of a goto statement is:
        goto label_name;
Here, label_name should be a valid identifier name, and : (colon) should be used after label_name.

86. Write a program to check login; a user can try for three times only.

```
#include<stdio.h>
#include<conio.h>
int main()
{
        char user_name='a',password='z',i=0;

        start:
                {
                printf("\nenter user_name");
                scanf("%c",&user_name);
                printf("\n\nenter password");
                password=getch();
                fflush(stdin);

                if(user_name!='a'||password!='z')
                  {
                  printf("\naccess denied\n");
                  goto incr;
                  }
                if(user_name=='a' && password=='z')
                  {
                printf("\nwelcome sir");
                  }

                goto end;
                }

        incr:
                { i++;
```

```c
            if(i<3)
              {
              goto start;
              }

            goto lock;

        }
lock:
        {
          printf("\naccount is locked");
          goto end;
        }

    end: getch();
}
```

8. Patterns

Pattern programs print various patterns of numbers and stars. These codes illustrate how to create various patterns using C programming.

Most of these C programs involve usage of nested for loops.
A pattern of numbers, stars, or characters is a way of arranging these in some logical manner, or they may form a sequence.

```
        For( ) // outer loop for rows
{
For( ) // inner loop for columns
{ }
}
```
The condition in the inner loop depends on the number of columns in a row.

87. Display the following pattern (26 pattern):

```
1)
*
**
***
****
******
```

```c
#include<stdio.h>
void main()
{
int i,j;
    for (i=1;i<=5;i++)
        {
                for(j=1;j<=i;j++)
                {
                printf("*");
                }
                printf("\n");
        }
}
```

2)
1
21
321
4321
54321

```
#include<stdio.h>
void main()
{
        for(i=1;i<=5;i++)
        {
                for(j=i;j>=1;j--)
                {
                printf("%d",j);
                }
                printf("\n");
        }
}
```

3)
54321
4321
321
21
1

```
#include<stdio.h>
void main()
{
        int i,j;
        for(i=5;i>=1;i--)
        {
                for(j=i;j>=1;j--)
                {
                printf("%d",j);
                }
                printf("\n");
        }
}
```

4)
54321
5432
543
54
5

```c
#include<stdio.h>
void main()
{
        int i,j;

            for(i=1;i<=5;i++)
                {
                        for(j=5;j>=i;j--)
                        {
                            printf("%d",j);
                        }
                            printf("\n");
                }
}
```

5)
12345
1234
123
12
1

```c
#include<stdio.h>
void main()
{
            int i,j;
                for(i=5;i>=1;i--)
                {
                        for(j=1;j<=i;j++)
                        {
                        printf("%d",j);
                        }
                        printf("\n");
                }
}
```

6)
```
*
*#
*#*
*#*#
*#*#*
```

```c
#include<stdio.h>
void main()
{
        int i,j;
        for(i=1;i<=5;i++)
        {
                for(j=1;j<=i;j++)
                {
                if(j%2==0)
                printf("#");
                else
                printf("*");
                }
                printf("\n");
        }
}
```

7)
```
5
54
543
5432
54321
```

```c
#include<stdio.h>
void main()
{
        int i,j;
        for(i=5;i>=1;i--)
        {
                for(j=1;j<i;j++)
                {
                        printf(" ");
                }
                for(j=5;j>=i;j--)
                {
```

```
                                        printf("%d",j);
                                    }
                                    printf("\n");
                    }
            }
```

8)
```
12345
 2345
  345
   45
    5
```

```c
#include<stdio.h>
void main()
{
            int i,j;
            for(i=1;i<=5;i++)
                    {
                    for(j=1;j<i;j++)
                    {
                            printf(" ");
                    }
                    for(j=i;j<=5;j++)
                            {
                                    printf("%d",j);
                            }
                            printf("\n");
                    }

            }
```

9)

```
    *
   **
  ***
 ****
*****
```

```c
#include<stdio.h>
void main()
{
            int i,j;
```

```
for(i=1;i<=5;i++)
{
        for(j=i;j<5;j++)
        {
                printf(" ");
        }
        for(j=1;j<=i;j++)
        {
                printf("*");
        }
        printf("\n");
}
}
```

10)
```
******
 ****
 ***
  **
  *
```

```
#include<stdio.h>
void main()
{
        int i,j;
        for (i=5;i>=1;i--)
        {
                for(j=5;j>i;j--)
                {
                        printf(" ");
                }
                for(j=1;j<=i;j++)
                {
                        printf("*");
                }
                printf("\n");
        }
}
```

11
```
    A
   BA
  CBA
 DCBA
EDCBA
```

```c
#include<stdio.h>

void main()
{
        int i,j;
        for(i=65;i<=69;i++)
        {
                for(j=i;j<69;j++)
                {
                printf(" ");
                }

                for(j=i;j>=65;j--)
                {
                printf("%c",j);
                }
                printf("\n");
        }
```

12)
```
    A
   AB
  ABC
 ABCD
ABCDE
```

```c
#include<stdio.h>
void main()
{
        int i,j;

    for (i=65;i<=69;i++)
        {
                for(j=i;j<69;j++)
                {
                printf(" ");
                }
```

```
                                                for(j=65;j<=i;j++)
                                                    {
                                                    printf("%c",j);
                                                    }
                                                printf("\n");
                                    }
                    }
```

13)
```
       A
      ABA
     ABCBA
    ABCDCBA
   ABCDEDCBA
```

```
            #include<stdio.h>
            void main()
            {

            int i,j,k;

                        for(i=65;i<=69;i++)
                            {
                                    for(j=i;j<69;j++)
                                    {
                                            printf(" ");
                                    }
                                    for(j=65;j<=i;j++)
                                    {
                                    printf("%c",j);
                                    }
                                    for(k=j–2;k>=65;k--)
                                        {
                                        printf("%c",k);
                                        }
                                        printf("\n");
                            }
                    }
```

14)
```
  *
 * *
* * *
 * * * *
* * * * *
```

```c
#include<stdio.h>
void main()
{

int i,j,k;

        for(i=1;i<=5;i++)
          {
                for(j=i;j<5;j++)
                {
                printf(" ");
                }
                for(j=1;j<=i;j++)
                {
                        if(j%2==0)
                        printf(" ");
                        else
                        printf("*");
                }
                for(k=j-2;k>=1;k--)
                        {
                        if(k%2==0)
                        printf(" ");
                        else
                        printf("*");
                        }
                        printf("\n");

          }
    }
```

15)
```
*********
 *******
  *****
   ***
    *
```

```c
#include<stdio.h>
void main()
{

int i,j,k;

        for(i=1;i<=5;i++)
        {
        for(j=1;j<i;j++)
         printf(" ");
        for(j=i;j<=5;j++)
         printf("*");
        for(k=i;k<5;k++)
         printf("*");

printf("\n");
        }
}
```

16.
```
_ _ _ _*
_ _ _ *_ *
_ _ *_ _ _ *
_* _ _ _ _ _*
*********
```

```c
#include <stdio.h>

int main()
{
   int i, j, rows=5;
   for(i=1; i<=rows; i++)
   {
      /* Print trailing spaces */
      for(j=i; j<rows; j++)
      {
         printf(" ");
      }
```

```c
        for(j=1; j<=(2*i-1); j++)
        {
    if(i==rows || j==1 || j==(2*i-1))
            {
                printf("*");
            }
            else
            {
                printf(" ");
            }
        }

        /* Move to next line */
        printf("\n");
    }

    return 0;
}
```

17.
```
*
* *
* * *
* * * *
* * * * *
* * * *
* * *
* *
*
```

```c
#include<stdio.h>

int main()
{
    int i, j, rows=5, columns;
    columns=1;

    for(i=1;i<rows*2;i++)
    {
        for(j=1; j<=columns; j++)
        {
            printf("*");
        }
```

```
        if(i < rows)
        {
                columns++;
        }
        else
        {
            columns--;
        }

    printf("\n");
    }

    return 0;
}
```

18.
```
* * * * * * * * *
* * * *     * * * *
* * *         * * *
* *             * *
*                 *
*                 *
* *               **
* * *         * * *
* * * *     * * * *
* * * * * * * * *
```

```c
#include <stdio.h>

int main()
{
    int i, j, n=5;

    for(i=1; i<=n; i++)
    {
        for(j=i; j<=n; j++)
        {
            printf("*");
        }

        for(j=1; j<=(2*i-2); j++)
        {
            printf(" ");
```

```
        }

    for(j=i; j<=n; j++)
    {
        printf("*");
    }

    printf("\n");
}

  for(i=1; i<=n; i++)
  {
    for(j=1; j<=i; j++)
    {
        printf("*");
    }


    for(j=(2*i-2); j<(2*n-2); j++)
    {
        printf(" ");
    }

    for(j=1; j<=i; j++)
    {
        printf("*");
    }

    printf("\n");
  }

    return 0;
}
```

19.
```
*       *
 *     *
  *   *
   *
  *   *
 *     *
*       *
```

```c
#include <stdio.h>

int main()
{
    int i, j, N=5;
    int count;

    count = N * 2 - 1;

    for(i=1; i<=count; i++)
    {
        for(j=1; j<=count; j++)
        {
            if(j==i || (j==count - i + 1))
            {
                printf("*");
            }
            else
            {
                printf(" ");
            }
        }

        printf("\n");
    }

    return 0;
}
```

20.
```
    *********
   *************
  ***************
 *****************
  *****************
   ***************
    *************
     ***********
      *********
       *******
        *****
         ***
          *
```

```c
#include <stdio.h>

int main()
{
    int i, j, n=10;

    for(i=n/2; i<=n; i+=2)
    {
        for(j=1; j<n-i; j+=2)
        {
            printf(" ");
        }

        for(j=1; j<=i; j++)
        {
            printf("*");
        }

        for(j=1; j<=n-i; j++)
        {
            printf(" ");
        }

        for(j=1; j<=i; j++)
        {
            printf("*");
        }
```

```
        printf("\n");
    }

    for(i=n; i>=1; i--)
    {
        for(j=i; j<n; j++)
        {
            printf(" ");
        }

        for(j=1; j<=(i*2)-1; j++)
        {
            printf("*");
        }

        printf("\n");
    }

    return 0;
}
```

21.
```
* * * *
 *     *
 *     *
 *     *
* * * *
```

```
#include <stdio.h>

int main()
{
    int i, j, rows=5;

    for(i=1; i<=rows; i++)
    {
        /* Print trailing spaces */
        for(j=1; j<=rows-i; j++)
        {
            printf(" ");
        }
```

```
/* Print stars and center spaces */
for(j=1; j<=rows; j++)
{
    if(i==1 || i==rows || j==1 || j==rows)
        printf("*");
    else
        printf(" ");
}

printf("\n");
}

return 0;
}
```

22.
```
56789
 4567
  345
   23
    1
```

```c
#include <stdio.h>

int main()
{
    int i, j, k, N=5;

    for(i=N; i>=1; i--)
    {
        k = i;

        for(j=1; j<=i; j++, k++)
        {
            printf("%d", k);
        }

        printf("\n");
    }

    return 0;
}
```

23.
```
1        1
12       21
123      321
1234    4321
1234554321
```

```c
#include <stdio.h>
int main()
{
    int i, j, N=5;
        for(i=1; i<=N; i++)
    {
        // Prints first part of pattern
        for(j=1; j<=i; j++)
        {
            printf("%d", j);
        }
        // Prints spaces between two parts
        for(j=i*2; j<N*2; j++)
        {
            printf(" ");
        }
        // Prints second part of the pattern
        for(j=i; j>=1; j--)
        {
            printf("%d", j);
        }

        printf("\n");
    }
    return 0;}
```

24.
```
1       1
2       2
 3     3
  4   4
   5
  4   4
 3     3
2       2
1       1
```

```c
#include <stdio.h>

int main()
{
    int i, j, N=5;

    // First part of the pattern
    for(i=1; i<=N; i++)
    {
        // Print trailing spaces
        for(j=1; j<i; j++)
        {
            printf(" ");
        }

        printf("%d", i);

        // Print central spacces
        for(j=1; j<=((N - i) * 2 - 1); j++)
        {
            printf(" ");
        }

        // Don't print for last row
        if(i != N)
            printf("%d", i);

        // Moves on to the next row
        printf("\n");
    }
```

```c
        // Second part of the pattern
        for(i=N-1; i>=1; i--)
        {
            // Print trailing spaces
            for(j=1; j<i; j++)
            {
                printf(" ");
            }

            printf("%d", i);

            // Print central spaces
            for(j=1; j<=((N - i ) * 2 - 1); j++)
            {
                printf(" ");
            }

            printf("%d", i);

            // Move on to the next line
            printf("\n");
        }

        return 0;
    }
```

25.
01110
10001
10001
10001
01110

```c
        #include <stdio.h>

        int main()
        {
            int i, j, rows=5, cols=5;

            for(i=1; i<=rows; i++)
            {
                for(j=1; j<=cols; j++)
                {
                    // Print corner element
```

```
         if((i==1 || i==rows) && (j==1 || j==cols))
         {
            printf("0");
         }
         else if(i==1 || i==rows || j==1 || j==cols)
         {   // Print edge
            printf("1");
         }
         else
         {    // Print center
            printf("0");
         }
      }

   printf("\n");
   }
   return 0;
}
```

26.
```
1
11
101
1001
11111
```

```
#include <stdio.h>

int main()
{
   int i, j, N=5;
   for(i=1; i<=N; i++)
   {
      for(j=1; j<=i; j++)
      {
         if(i==1 || i==N || j==1 || j==i)
         {
            printf("1");
         }
         else
         {
            printf("0");
         }
```

```
        }

        printf("\n");
    }

    return 0;
}
```

88. Write a program to convert a decimal number into a binary number.

```c
#include <stdio.h>

int main()
{
    long decimal, temp, binary;
    int rem, place = 1;

    binary = 0;

    printf("Enter any decimal number: ");
    scanf("%lld", &decimal);

    temp = decimal;

    /* Decimal to binary conversion */
    while(temp > 0)
    {
        rem = temp % 2;

        binary = (rem * place) + binary;

        temp /= 2;

        place *= 10;
    }

    printf("Decimal number = %ld\n", decimal);
    printf("Binary number = %ld", binary);

    return 0;
}
```

89. Write a program to count the number of times a digit occurs in a number.

```c
#include <stdio.h>
int main()
{
    long num, n;
    int i, LDigit;
    int freq[10];

    printf("Enter any number: ");
    scanf("%ld", &num);

    /* Initialize frequency array with 0 */
    for(i=0; i<10; i++)
    {
        freq[i] = 0;
    }

    /* Copy the value of 'num' to 'n' */
    n = num;

    /* Run till 'n' is not equal to zero */
    while(n != 0)
    {
        /* Get last digit */
        LDigit = n % 10;
        n /= 10;

        /* Increment frequency array */
        freq[LDigit]++;
    }

    printf("Frequency of each digit in %ld is: \n", num);
    for(i=0; i<10; i++)
    {
        printf("Frequency of %d = %d\n", i, freq[i]);
    }

    return 0;
}
```

90. Write a program to input 10 numbers in an array and print it in the reverse order.

```
#include <stdio.h>
void main()
{
  int i,n,a[10];

  printf("Input %d number of elements in the array :\n",n);
  for(i=0;i<10;i++)
    {
        printf("element - %d : ",i);
        scanf("%d",&a[i]);
    }

  printf("\nThe values store into the array are : \n");
  for(i=0;i<10;i++)
    {
        printf("% 5d",a[i]);
    }

  printf("\n\nThe values store into the array in reverse are :\n");
  for(i=9;i>=0;i--)
    {
        printf("% 5d",a[i]);
    }
    printf("\n\n");
}
```

91. Write a program to print the sum of elements in an array.

```
#include<stdio.h>
#include<conio.h>
int main()
{
int a[5],i,sum=0;
        for(i=0;i<5;i++)
        {
        printf("enter %d number",i+1);
        scanf("%d",&a[i]);
        }
        for(i=0;i<5;i++)
        {
        printf("\na[%d]=%d",i,a[i]);
```

```
                sum=sum+a[i];
                }
                        printf("\nsum of array=%d",sum);
                        return1;

        }
```

92. Write a program to check whether an element exists in an array or not (linear search)

```
        #include<stdio.h>
        #include<conio.h>
        int main()
        {
        int a[5],i,sum=0,v,position=-1;
        for(i=0;i<5;i++)
                {
                        printf("enter %d number",i+1);
                        scanf("%d",&a[i]);

                }
                        printf("\nenter a number to search");
                        scanf("%d",&v);

        for(i=0;i<5;i++)
                {
                        if(v==a[i])
                                {

                                position=i+1;
                                break;
                                }
                                }

                        if(position==-1)
                        {
                        printf("\nvalue does not exist");

                        }
                        else

                        printf("\n value exist at position
                        %d",position);

                        return 1;

        }
```

9.Using string.h

A string in the C language is simply an array of characters. Strings must have a NULL or \0 character after the last character to show where the string ends. A string can be declared as a character array or with a string pointer.

The C language provides no explicit support for strings in the language itself. The string-handling functions are implemented in libraries.

String I/O operations are implemented in <stdio.h> (puts, gets, etc.). A set of simple string manipulation functions is implemented in <string.h>, or on some systems in <strings.h>.

The string library (string.h or strings.h) has some useful functions for working with strings, such as strcpy, strcat, strcmp, strlen, and strcoll. We will take a look at some of these string operations.

String functions	Description
strcat ( )	Concatenates str2 at the end of str1
strncat ( )	Appends a portion of string to another
strcpy ( )	Copies str2 into str1
strncpy ( )	Copies the given number of characters of one string to another
strlen ( )	Gives the length of str1
strcmp ( )	Returns 0 if str1 is same as str2. Returns <0 if str1 < str2. Returns >0 if str1 > str2
strcmpi ( )	Same as strcmp() function. But, this function negotiates case. "A" and "a" are treated as same.
strchr ( )	Returns pointer to the first occurrence of char in str1
strrchr ( )	Last occurrence of a given character in a string is found
strstr ( )	Returns pointer to the first occurrence of str2 in str1
strrstr ( )	Returns pointer to the last occurrence of str2 in str1
strdup ( )	Duplicates the string

strlwr ( )	Converts a string to lowercase
strupr ( )	Converts a string to uppercase
strrev ( )	Reverses the given string
strset ( )	Sets all character in a string to a given character
strnset ( )	It sets the portion of characters in a string to the given character
strtok ( )	Tokenizes the given string using a delimiter

93. Write a program to merge a title according to the gender in name using the string.h function.

```
void main(){
int i;
    char a[20],b[20];

  char gender;

        printf("enter your name");
        scanf("%s",&a);
        fflush(stdin);
        printf("enter your gender");
        scanf("%c",&gender);

            if(gender=='m'||gender=='M')
            {
            //printf("Mr. %s",a);
            strcpy(b,"Mr.");
            }
            else
            {
            //printf("Ms. %s",a);
            strcpy(b,"Ms.");
            }
            strcat(b,a);
            printf("%s",b);

            }}
```

94. Write a program to enter a one-digit number and display it in words.

```
#include<stdio.h>
void main()
{
char n[][10]={{"Zero"},{"one"},{"two"},{"three"},{"four"},{"f
ive"},{"six"},{"seven"},{"eight"},{"nine"}};
int num;
printf("enter any 1 digit number \n");
scanf("%d",&num);

        printf("\nIn Words: %s",n[num]);

}
```

10. Array– 1D and 2D

An array is a collection of similar data type values.

An array is defined as a finite-ordered collection of homogenous data, stored in continuous memory locations.

The syntax of an array is:

> Datatype array_name[size]; // 1D array
> Datatype array_name[No_of_Rows][No-Of_columns] // 2D array

An array index always starts with 0 to size–1. Both the row and column index starts with 0.

Advantages of arrays

1) Code optimization: Less code to access the data.
2) Easy to traverse data: By using the for loop, we can retrieve the elements of an array easily.
3) Easy to sort/search data: To sort the elements of an array, we just need a few lines of code.
4) Random access: We can access any element randomly using an array.

95. Write a program to copy the elements from one array into another.

```
#include <stdio.h>

void main()
{
   int arr1[10], arr2[10];
   int i, n;

   for(i=0;i<10;i++)
   {
         printf("element - %d : ",i);
         scanf("%d",&arr1[i]);
   }
   /* Copy elements of first array into second array.*/
   for(i=0; i<10; i++)
   {
     arr2[i] = arr1[i];
   }

   /* Prints the elements of first array   */
```

```
printf("\nThe elements stored in the first array are :\n");
for(i=0; i<n; i++)
{
    printf("% 5d", arr1[i]);
}

/* Prints the elements copied into the second array. */
printf("\n\nThe elements copied into the second array are :\n");
for(i=0; i<n; i++)
{
    printf("% 5d", arr2[i]);
}
            printf("\n\n");
}
```

96. Write a program to find the maximum, second maximum, sum of even, and sum of odd elements of an array.

```
#include<stdio.h>
void main()
{
int a[5],i,max,smax=0,ev=0,od=0;
        for(i=0;i<5;i++)
        {
        printf("Enter no\n");
        scanf("%d",&a[i]);
        }
        max=a[0];
        smax=a[0];

        for(i=1;i<5;i++)
        {
        if(a[i]>max)
         max=a[i];
        else if(a[i]>smax )
                smax=a[i];

        if(a[i]%2==0)
         ev=ev+a[i];
        else
```

```
od=od+a[i];

}
printf("\nMaximum=%d\nsecond maximum=%d\nsum
of even=%d\nsum of odd=%d",max,smax,ev,od);
}
```

97. Write a program to enter the first alphabet of your name and print a pattern.

```
Hint: Input: A
A
AB
ABC
ABCD
ABCDE

#include<stdio.h>
void main()
{
int i,j;
char c;
        printf("Enter 1st letter of your name");
        scanf("%c",&c);
for(i=c;i<=c+5;i++)
{
for(j=c;j<=i;j++)
{
        printf("%c",j);
}
printf("\n");
}
}
```

98. Write a program to convert a decimal into binary or octal number.

```
#include<stdio.h>
#include<conio.h>
#include<math.h>
void main()
{
        int n,r,a[8],i=0,j,x;

        printf("\nenter any decimal number");
        scanf("%d",&n);
```

```
            printf("\npress 2 for binary & 8 for octal");
            scanf("%d",&x);
            while(n>=x)
            {
                    r=n%x;
                    a[i++]=r;
                    n=n/x;

            }
            if(n>0)
            a[i++]=n;
            for(j=i–1;j>=0;j--)
            printf("%d",a[j]);
    }
```

99. Write a program to convert a binary/octal number into a decimal number.

```
    #include<stdio.h>
    #include<conio.h>
    #include<math.h>
    void main()
    {
    int n,r,x,y=0,i=0,z;
            printf("press 2 for binary and press 8 for octal");
            scanf("%d",&z);
            printf("enter binary/octal num");
            scanf("%d",&n);
            while(n!=0)
            {
                    r=n%10;
                    x=r*pow(z,i++);
                    y=y+x;
                    n=n/10;

            }
                    printf("decimal number is=%d",y);

    }
```

100. Write a program to sort an array in ascending order (linear sorting).

```c
#include<stdio.h>
int main()
{
int a[5],i=0,j,temp;
    for(i=0;i<5;i++)
        {
        printf("Enter value\n");
        scanf("%d",&a[i]);
        }
for(i=0;i<5;i++)
        {
        for(j=i+1;j<5;j++)
        {
        if(a[i]>a[j])
        {
        temp=a[i];
        a[i]=a[j];
        a[j]=temp;
        }
        }
        }
printf("\nSorted array:\n");
        for(i=0;i<5;i++)
        {
        printf("\n%d",a[i]);
        }
}
```

101. Write a program to sort an array using bubble sort.

```c
#include<stdio.h>
int main()
{
int a[5],i=0,j,temp;
        printf("\n\n--Bubble Sorting----\n\n");
        for(i=0;i<5;i++)
        {
        printf("Enter value\n");
        scanf("%d",&a[i]);
        }
```

```
for(i=0;i<5;i++)
{
for(j=0;j<5-i-1;j++)
{
if(a[j]>a[j+1])
{
temp=a[j];
a[j]=a[j+1];
a[j+1]=temp;
}
}
}
printf("\nSorted array:\n");
for(i=0;i<5;i++)
{
printf("\n%d",a[i]);
}
}
```

102. Write a program to search a value in an array using binary search.

```
#include<stdio.h>
int main()
{
int a[5],i=0,j,temp,first=0,last=4,mid,v,pos=-1;

for(i=0;i<5;i++)
{
printf("Enter value\n");
scanf("%d",&a[i]);
}

printf("\nEntre value to search");
scanf("%d",&v);

while(first<last)
{
mid=(first+last)/2;
if(a[mid]==v)
{
pos=mid+1;
break;
}
if(a[mid]>v)
```

```
                    {
                    last=mid–1;
                    }
                    if(a[mid]<v)
                    {
                    first=mid+1;
                    }
                    }

                    if(pos==–1)
                     printf("\nval not found ");
                    else
                     printf("\nval found at position %d",pos);
            }
```

103. Write a program to enter your name and display a pattern.

```
            Hint: Hello
            H
            He
            Hel
            Hell
            Hello
            #include<stdio.h>
            int main()
            {
                    int i,j;
                    char a[20];
                                    printf("enter your name");
                                    scanf("%s",a);
                            for(i=0;a[i]!=NULL;i++)
                            {
                                    for(j=0;j<=i;j++)
                                    {
                                    printf("%c",a[j]);
                                    }

                                    printf("\n");
                    }

            }
```

104. Write a program to count the vowels in a given name.

```
#include<stdio.h>
int main()
{
char a[20];
int i,count=0;
        printf("enter your name");
        gets(a);
        for(i=0;a[i]!=NULL;i++)
        {
            if(a[i]=='a'||a[i]=='e'||a[i]=='i'||a[i]=='o'||a[i]=='u')
                {
                count++;
                }
        }
        printf("number of vowel are %d",count);
}
```

105. Write a program to enter a string and replace *a* with *e*.

```
#include<stdio.h>
int main()
{
            int i;
            char a[20];
            printf("enter your name");
            gets(a);

            for(i=0;a[i]!=NULL;i++)
            {
            if(a[i]=='a')
            a[i]='e';
            if(a[i]=='A')
            a[i]='E';
}
Printf("\n%s",a);
            }
```

105. Write a program to convert a capital letter into small and vice-versa in a given string.

```c
#include<stdio.h>
void main()
{
char n[20];
int i;
printf("Entre name");
gets(n);

printf("\nHello %s\n",n);

printf("\n\n%s",n);
for(i=0;n[i]!='\0';i++)
{
        if(n[i]>=65 && n[i]<=90)
        n[i]+=32;
        else if(n[i]>=97 && n[i]<=122)
        n[i]-=32;
}
printf("\n\n\n%s",n);
}
```

106. Write a program to print the initials(abbreviation) of a given name.

```c
#include<stdio.h>
#include<conio.h>
int main()
{
                int i;
                char n[50];

                        printf("enter your name");
                        gets(n);
                        printf("\n\n");
printf("%c.",n[0]);
                        for(i=1;n[i]!=NULL;i++)
                        {
                        if(n[i]==' ')
                        printf("%c.",n[i+1]);
                        }
return 1;
}
```

107. Write a program to calculate the space and print the length of a name, excluding spaces.

```
#include<stdio.h>
#include<conio.h>
int main()
{
        int i,count=0;
        char n[50];

            printf("enter your name");
            //scanf("%s",n);
            gets(n);
            printf("\n\n");
            for(i=0;n[i]!=NULL;i++)
            {
                    if(n[i]==' ')
                    count++;

            }
            printf("\n");

            printf("\nSpace in name are %d",count);
            printf("\n\n");
        printf("\nLength of name exclding spaces is %d"i–
count);

    return 1;
    }
```

108. Write a program to convert an upper-case letter into lower-case and vice-versa in a given name.

```
#include<stdio.h>
#include<conio.h>
int main()
{
        int i,count=0;
        char n[50];

            printf("enter your name");
            //scanf("%s",n);
            gets(n);
```

```
                                    printf("\n\n");
                                    for(i=0;n[i]!=NULL;i++)
                                    {
                                            if(n[i]>=65 && n[i]<=90)
                                            n[i]+=32;
                                            else if(n[i]>=97 && n[i]<=122)
                                            n[i]=n[i]-32;
                                    }
                        puts(n);
                                    printf("\n");

                return 1;
        }
```

109. Write a program to print a name in the reverse order.

```
        #include<conio.h>
        int main()
        {
                        int i,j;
                        char n[50];

                                    printf("enter your name");
                                    //scanf("%s",n);
                                    gets(n);
                                    printf("\n\n");

                                    for(i=0;n[i]!=NULL;i++); //length of
                                    name

                                    for(j=i-1;j>=0;j--)
                                    {
                                    printf("%c",n[j]);
                        }

                                    printf("\n");

                return 1;
                }
```

110. Write a program to check whether a given name is palindrome or not.

```
Hint: original string = reverse string
#include<stdio.h>
#include<conio.h>
#include<string.h>
int main()
{
char a[10],b[10];
int x;
        printf("Enter name");
        scanf("%s",a);

strcpy(b,a);
        printf("\ncopy of a into b %s",b);

        strrev(a);
printf("\nReverse a %s",a);

        if(x==0)
                printf("\nPalindrome string");
        else
                printf("\nNot palindrome");
return 1;
}
```

111. Usingthe string function using string.h

```
#include<conio.h>
#include<string.h>
int main()
{
char a[10],b[10],c[10]={"Hello "};
int i,len,x;
        printf("Enter name");
        scanf("%s",a);
        len=strlen(a);
        printf("\nLength of name is %d",len);
        strcpy(b,a);
        printf("\ncopy of a into b %s",b);
        strupr(b);
        printf("\nCapitalize b %s",b);
        strlwr(b);
        printf("\nIn Small letters b= %s",b);
        strrev(a);
```

```
                    printf("\nReverse a %s",a);
                    x=strcmp(a,b);
                            if(x==0)
                             printf("\nPalindrome string");
                            else
                             printf("\nNot palindrome");
                    strcat(c,b);
                    printf("\nConcatenate c %s",c);
            return 1;
            }
```

112. Write a program to find the roll number of a student out of 10 students, scoring the highest marks.

```
                #include<stdio.h>
                int main()
                {
                        int a[10][2],i,j,rn,max=0;
                            for(i=0;i<10;i++)
                            {
                                    printf("enter roll no. and marks");
                                    for(j=0;j<2;j++)
                                    {
                                            scanf("%d",&a[i][j]);
                                    }

                            }
                            printf("\nroll no\t marks\n");
                            for(i=0;i<10;i++)
                                {
                                        for(j=0;j<2;j++)
                                        {
                                        printf("%d\t",a[i][j]);

                                        }
                                    printf("\n");
                                }

                        for(i=0;i<10;i++)
                        {
                                if(a[i][1]>max)
                                {
                                max=a[i][1];
                                rn=a[i][0];
                                }
```

```
                }
                    printf("\nroll no %d scored highest marks
%d",rn,max);
                }
```

113. Write a program to input a 3×3 matrix and print the sum of rows.

```
#include<stdio.h>
int main()
{
int a[3][3],i,j,sum_row;
        for(i=0;i<3;i++)
            {
            printf("\nenter 3 nos");
            for(j=0;j<3;j++)
                {
                scanf("%d",&a[i][j]);
        }
        }
        for(i=0;i<3;i++)
                {
                printf("\n");
                sum_row=0;

                for(j=0;j<3;j++)
                {
                printf("%d\t",a[i][j]);
                sum_row= sum_row+a[i][j];
        }
        printf("=%d", sum_row);
        }
        getch();
            }
```

114. Write a program to input a 3×3 matrix and print the transpose matrix.

```
#include<stdio.h>
int main()
{
int a[3][3],i,j;
        for(i=0;i<3;i++)
            {
            printf("\nenter 3 nos");
            for(j=0;j<3;j++)
```

```
        {
        scanf("%d",&a[i][j]);
}
}
for(i=0;i<3;i++)
        {
        printf("\n");
        for(j=0;j<3;j++)
        {
        printf("%d\t",a[j][i]);
}
}

}
```

115. Write a program to input a 3×3 matrix and print the diagonal of the matrix.

```
#include<stdio.h>
int main()
{
int a[3][3],i,j;
        for(i=0;i<3;i++)
        {
        printf("\nenter 3 nos");
        for(j=0;j<3;j++)
        {
        scanf("%d",&a[i][j]);
}
}
for(i=0;i<3;i++)
        {
        printf("\n");

        printf("%d\t",a[i][i]);
}

}
```

116.Write a program to input two 3×3 matrices and print their multiplication.

```
#include<stdio.h>

int main() {
  int a[3][3], b[3][3], c[3][3], i, j, k;
  int sum = 0;

  printf("\nEnter First Matrix : n");
  for (i = 0; i < 3; i++) {
    for (j = 0; j < 3; j++) {
      scanf("%d", &a[i][j]);
    }
  }

  printf("\nEnter Second Matrix:n");
  for (i = 0; i < 3; i++) {
    for (j = 0; j < 3; j++) {
      scanf("%d", &b[i][j]);
    }
  }

  printf("The First Matrix is: \n");
  for (i = 0; i < 3; i++) {
    for (j = 0; j < 3; j++) {
      printf(" %d ", a[i][j]);
    }
    printf("\n");
  }

  printf("The Second Matrix is : \n");
  for (i = 0; i < 3; i++) {
    for (j = 0; j < 3; j++) {
      printf(" %d ", b[i][j]);
    }
    printf("\n");
  }

  //Multiplication Logic
  for (i = 0; i <= 2; i++) {
    for (j = 0; j <= 2; j++) {
      sum = 0;
      for (k = 0; k <= 2; k++) {
        sum = sum + a[i][k] * b[k][j];
      }
```

```
        c[i][j] = sum;
      }
  }

  printf("\nMultiplication Of Two Matrices : \n");
  for (i = 0; i < 3; i++) {
    for (j = 0; j < 3; j++) {
      printf(" %d ", c[i][j]);
    }
    printf("\n");
  }

  return (0);
}
```

117. Write a program to input two 3×3 matrices and print the addition of both matrices.

```
#include<stdio.h>

int main()
{
    int arr1[3][3], arr2[3][3], arr3[3][3];
    int i, j;
    printf("Enter First 3*3 Matrix Elements:\n");
    for(i = 0; i < 3; i++)
    {
        for(j = 0; j < 3; j++)
        {
            scanf("%d", &arr1[i][j]);
        }
    }
    printf("\nEnter Second 3*3 Matrix Elements:\n");
    for(i = 0; i < 3; i++)
    {
        for(j = 0; j < 3; j++)
        {
            scanf("%d", &arr2[i][j]);
        }
    }
    printf("\nAddition of Matrices:\n");
    for(i = 0; i < 3; i++)
    {
```

```
        for(j = 0; j < 3; j++)
        {
            arr3[i][j] = arr1[i][j] + arr2[i][j];
        }
    }
    printf("\nThird Matrix Elements:\n");
    for(i = 0; i < 3; i++)
    {
        for(j = 0; j < 3; j++)
        {
            printf("%d\t", arr3[i][j]);
        }
        printf("\n");
    }
    printf("\n");
    return 0;
}
```

118. Write a program in C to accept a matrix and determine whether it is a sparse matrix.

```
#include <stdio.h>

/*A sparse martix is matrix which  has more zero elements than
nonzero elements */
void main ()
{
        static int arr1[10][10];
        int i,j,r,c;
        int ctr=0;
    printf("Input the number of rows of the matrix : ");
    scanf("%d", &r);
    printf("Input the number of columns of the matrix : ");
    scanf("%d", &c);

        printf("Input elements in the first matrix :\n");
    for(i=0;i<r;i++)
    {
        for(j=0;j<c;j++)
        {
                printf("element - [%d],[%d] : ",i,j);
                scanf("%d",&arr1[i][j]);
                    if (arr1[i][j]==0)
                    {
```

```
                               ++ctr;
                           }
                   }
            }
            if (ctr>((r*c)/2))
            {
                    printf ("The given matrix is sparse matrix. \n");
            }
            else
                    printf ("The given matrix is not a sparse
matrix.\n");

            printf ("There are %d number of zeros in the matrix.\n\
n",ctr);
}
```

119. Write a pogram to find whether a given number exists in an array or not
(binary search).

```
#inilude <stdio.h>

int main()
{
    int i, first, last, middle,search, array[10],pos=–1;

    for (i = 0; i < 10; i++)
      scanf("%d",&array[i]);

    printf("Enter value to find\n");
    scanf("%d", &search);

    first = 0;
    last = n –1;
    middle = (first+last)/2;

    while (first <= last) {
      if (array[middle] < search)
        first = middle + 1;
      else if (array[middle] == search) {
        pos=middle+1;
          break;
      }
      else
        last = middle –1;
```

```
        middle = (first + last)/2;
    }
    if (pos==-1)
        printf("Not found! %d is not present in the list.\n", search);
    else
        printf("\nvalue found at position =%d",pos);
    return 0;
}
```

120. Write a program in C to find the maximum occurring character in a string.

```c
#include <stdio.h>
#include <string.h>
#include <stdlib.h>

#define str_size 100 //Declare the maximum size of the string
#define chr_no 255 //Maximum number of characters to be
allowed

void main()
{
    char str[str_size];
        int ch_fre[chr_no];
    int i = 0, max;
    int ascii;

        printf("\n\nFind maximum occurring character in a string
:\n");
        printf("-------------------------------------------------\n");
        printf("Input the string : ");
        fgets(str, sizeof str, stdin);

    for(i=0; i<chr_no; i++)  //Set frequency of all characters to 0
    {
        ch_fre[i] = 0;
    }

    /* Read for frequency of each characters */
    i=0;
    while(str[i] != '\0')
    {
        ascii = (int)str[i];
        ch_fre[ascii] += 1;

        i++;
```

```
        }
    max = 0;
    for(i=0; i<chr_no; i++)
    {
        if(i!=32)
        {
        if(ch_fre[i] > ch_fre[max])
            max = i;
        }
    }
    printf("The Highest frequency of character '%c' appears
number of times : %d \n\n", max, ch_fre[max]);
}
```

11. Functions – call by value / call by reference

A function is a block of code that performs a specific task. Every C program has at least one function, which ismain().

Depending on whether a function is defined by the user or already included in C compilers, there are two types of functions in C programming:

- Standard library functions
- User-defined functions

The *standard library functions* are built-in functions in C programming to handle tasks such as mathematical computations, I/O processing, and string handling.

These functions are defined in the header file. When you include the header file, these functions are available for use.

C allows programmers to define functions. Such functions created by the user are called as*user-defined functions*.

Depending on the complexity and requirement of the program, one can create as many user-defined functions as one wants.

Advantages of user-defined functions:

- The program is easier to understand, maintain, and debug.
- Reusable codecan be used in other programs.
- A large program can be divided into smaller modules. Hence, a large project can be divided among many programmers.

Creatinga user-defined function

The four factors must be considered when creating a user-defined function:

- Prototype/declaration
- Definition/body
- Call
- Return type

Prototype

A prototype can occur at the top of a C source code file to describe what the function returns and what it takes (return type and parameter list).

When this is the case (occurring at the top of the file), the function prototype should be followed by a semicolon.

Return_type function_name(Argument list...);

Definition

Every function should have a task to perform. Definition should match with prototype.

Return_type function_name(argument list..){}

Call

When one piece of code invokes or calls a function, the number of args "passed" into a function must exactly match the number of parameters required for the function.

The type of each argument must exactly match the type of each parameter. The return variable type must exactly match the return type of the function.

Variable=function_name(argument..);

Return type

When a line of code in a function that says: "return X;" is executed, the function "ends" and no more code in the function is executed.

The value of X (or the value in the variable represented by X) becomes the result of the function.

Argument/Parameter

A parameter is the symbolic name for "data" that goes into a function. There are two ways to pass parameters in C: pass by value and pass by reference.

- Pass by value

Pass by value means that a copy of the data is made and stored by way of the name of the parameter.

Any changes to the parameter have *no* effect on data in the calling function.

- Pass by reference

A reference parameter "refers" to the original data in the calling function.

Thus, any changes made to the parameter cause a *change to the original variable.*

Void functions

If a function does not return a value, then a special "TYPE" is used to inform this to the computer. The return type is "void".

121. Write a function to display the addition of given two numbers.

```
#include<stdio.h>
void addition(int ,int);
voidaddition(int a,int b)
{
        int c=a+b;
        printf("\nAddition=%d",c);
}
void main()
{
int a,b;
        printf("Enter 2 nos");
        scanf("%d%d ",&a,&b);
                addition(a,b);
}
```

122. Write a function to calculate x=(a*b)+10.

```
#include<stdio.h>
# define max 10

void addi(int ,int);
int multi(int,int);
void addi(int a,int b)
{
        int c=a+b;
        printf("\nAddition=%d",c);
}
int multi(int a,int b)
{
        int d=a*b;
        return(d);
}
void main()
{
int a,b, x;
        printf("Enter 2 nos");
        scanf("%d%d ",&a,&b);
        x=multi(a,b);
        addi(x,max);
}
```

123. Write a function to calculate the factorial of given number.

```
#include<stdio.h>
int fact(int);
int fact(int n)
{
        int i,f=1;
        for(i=1;i<=n;i++)
        {
        f=f*i;
        }
        return(f);
}
int main()
{
        int n,f;
                printf("enter a no");
                scanf("%d",&n);

        f-fact(n);
        printf("\nFactorial of %d is %d",n,f);
}
```

124. Write a program to find the sum of the series 1!/1+2!/2+3!/3+4!/4+5!/5 ... !n/n using the user defined function

```
#include<stdio.h>
int fact(int);
int fact(int n)
{
        int i,f=1;
        for(i=1;i<=n;i++)
        {
        f=f*i;
        }
        return(f);
}
int main()
{/*factorial sum*/
        int n,f,i,sum=0;
                printf("enter a no");
                scanf("%d",&n);
                for(i=1;i<=n;i++)
                {
```

```
                    f=fact(i)/i;
                    sum=sum+f;
                    }
                    printf("%d",sum);
                    return(1);

        }
```

125. Write a program to calculate {{(a+b)*(c+d)}+{(e+f)*(g+h)}} using user defined function.

```
            #include<stdio.h>
            int addi(int,int);
            int multi(int,int);
            int addi(int a,int b)
            {
                    int x;
                    x=a+b;
                    return(x);

            }
            int multi(int c,int d)
            {
                    int x;
                    x=c*d;
                    return(x);

            }
            int main()
            {
                    int a,b,c,d,e,f,g,h,x;
                    printf("enter 8 values");
                    scanf("%d%d%d%d%d%d%d%d",&a,&b,&c,&d,&e,&f
            ,&g,&h);
                    x=sum((multi(sum(a,b),sum(c,d))),(multi(sum(e,f),sum(
            g,h))));
                    printf("%d",x);
            return(1);
            }
```

126. Write a program to check whether a given number is palindrome or not; create a function to reverse the number.

```c
#include<stdio.h>
int reverse();
int input_int();
int input_int()
{
        int n;
        printf("enter a number");
        scanf("%d",&n);
        return(n);
}
int reverse(int n)
{
        int r,s=0;
        while(n!=0)
        {
        r=n%10;
        n=n/10;
        s=s*10+r;
        }
        return(s);

}
int main()
{
        int a,x;

                a=input_int();
                x=reverse(a);
                if(x==a)
                {
                printf("number is palindrome");
                }
                else
                {
                printf("not a palindrome number");
                }

}
```

127. Write a program to calculate the area of a circle, and create a function for PI() and square().

```
#include<stdio.h>
float pi();
float pi()
{
        return(3.14);
}
int square(int w)
{
        return(w*w);
}
void main()
{
        int r;
        float x,area;
        printf("enter radius");
        scanf("%d",&r);
        x=pi();
        //area=(x*r*r);
        area=pi()*square(r);
        printf("area of circle with radius %d is %5.2f",r,area);

}
```

128. Write a program to separate every message by line of the star. Create a function to print the star.

```
#include<stdio.h>
void input_star()
{
        printf("\n********************\n");
}
int main()
{
        input_star();
        input_star();
        printf("good morning");
        input_star();
        printf("good after noon");
        input_star();
        printf("good evening");
        input_star();
```

```
printf("good night ");
input_star();
input_star();
}
```

129. Write a program to create all functions of an ATM.

```
#include<stdio.h>
#include<conio.h>
#include<string.h>
#include<stdlib.h>
int main()
{
char c;
int i,temp=1,amt=10000,ch,rs;
        printf("\nEnter 4 digit ATM pin\n");
        for(i=0;i<4;i++)
        {
        c=getch();
        printf("*");
        if(c!='0')
        {
         temp=0;
         break;
        }
        }
        if(temp==0)
         printf("\nInvalid pin.Pleasetry again");
        else
         {
        printf("\nWelcome user\n");
        while(1)
        {
        printf("\nWhat do you want?\npress 1 for withdraw\
        npress 2 for deposit\npress 3 for check balance\npress 4
        for Logout\n");
        scanf("%d",&ch);
         switch(ch)
         {
        case 1:
                printf("\nEnter amount to withdraw\n");
                scanf("%d",&rs);
                if(rs>amt)
```

```
                      {
                      printf("insufficient balance");
                      }
                      else
                      {
                      amt=amt–rs;
                      printf("\nPleasecollect your amount..\
                      nBalance=%d",amt);
                      }
                      break;
            case 2:
                      printf("\nEnter amount to withdraw\n");
                      scanf("%d",&rs);
                      amt=amt+rs;
                      printf("\nBalance=%d",amt);
                      break;
            case 3:
                      printf("\nyou have %d Rs. in
                      balance",amt);
                      break;
            case 4:
                      exit(0);

            }
            }
      }

      return 1;
      }
```

130. Write a program to swap two numbers.

```
            #include<stdio.h>
            void interchange(int,int);
                  int main()
                  {
                              int a,b;
                              printf("enter 2 nos");
                              scanf("%d%d",&a,&b);

                              interchange(a,b);
                              printf("\nAfter change in main() a=%d,
                              b=%d",a,b);
```

```
                return 1;
        }
        void interchange(int a,int b)
        {
                int c=a;
                a=b;
                b=c;
        printf("\nAfter change in interchange() a=%d,
        b=%d",a,b);
        }
```

131. Write a program to swap two numbers using a pointer.

```
        #include<stdio.h>
        void interchange(int,int);
        void swap(int *,int *);
                int main()
                {
                        int a,b;
                        printf("enter 2 nos");
                        scanf("%d%d",&a,&b);

                        interchange(a,b);
                        printf("\nAfter change in main() a=%d,
                        b=%d",a,b);

                        swap(&a,&b);
                        printf("\nAfter swap in main() a=%d,
                        b=%d",a,b);
                        return 1;
                }
        void interchange(int a,int b)
        {
                int c=a;
                a=b;
                b=c;
                printf("\nAfter change in interchange() a=%d,
                b=%d",a,b);
        }
        void swap(int *a,int *b)
        {
                int c=(*a);
                (*a)=(*b);
```

```
                    (*b)=c;
        printf("\nAfter change in swap() a=%d, b=%d",*a,*b);
        }
```

132. Write a program to calculate the factorial of given number using recursion.

```
#include<conio.h>
int fact(int n)
{
static int f=1;
        if(n==1)
         return 1;
        else
         f=n*fact(n-1);

return(f);
}
void main()
{
int n,f;
        printf("Enter a number");
        scanf("%d",&n);
        f=fact(n);
        printf("\nFactorial=%d",f);
getch();
}
```

133. Write a program to find the largest element of an array using the function.

```
#include<stdio.h>

int findMaxElem(int []);
int n;

int main()
{
   int arr1[10],mxelem,i;

     printf(" Input %d elements in the array :\n",n);
     for(i=0;i<10;i++)
      {
             printf(" element - %d : ",i);
             scanf("%d",&arr1[i]);
      }
```

```
mxelem=findMaxElem(arr1);

printf(" The largest element in the array is : %d\n\n",mxelem);
return 0;
}
int findMaxElem(int arr1[])
{
   int i=1,mxelem;
   mxelem=arr1[0];
   while(i < 10)
        {
    if(mxelem<arr1[i])
       mxelem=arr1[i];
    i++;
    }
    return mxelem;
}
```

134. Write a program to display the calculator menu.

```
#include <stdio.h>
#include <stdlib.h>

void displaymenu(){

printf("          MENU          \n");

printf("===============================\n");
            printf("   1.Add\n");


            printf("   2.Subtract \n");

            printf("   3.Multiply \n");

            printf("   4.Divide \n");

            printf("   5.Modulus \n");

                                    }

        int Add(int a,int b){

                        return(a+b);
```

```
                                              }
          int Substract(int a, int b){

                                      return(a–b);
                              }
                int Multiply(int a, int b){

                                              return(a*b);
                      }
          float Divide(int a,int b){

                                              return(a/b);

          }
                int Modulus(int a, int b){

                                              return(a%b);

                                                              }

          int main()
          {
          //show menu
          displaymenu();
          int yourchoice;
          int a;
          int b;
          char confirm;
                  do
                          {
                          printf("Enter your choice(1-5):");
                          scanf("%d:",&yourchoice);
                          printf("Enter your two integer numbers:");
                          scanf("%d %d",&a,&b);
                          printf("\n");
                          switch(yourchoice)
          {
                  case 1:
          printf("Result:%d",Add(a,b));break;
                  case 2:
          printf("Result:%d",Substract(a,b));break;
                  case 3:
          printf("Result:%d",Multiply(a,b));break;
                  case 4:
```

```
printf("Result:%.2f",Divide(a,b));break;
        case 5:
printf("Result:%d",Modulus(a,b));break;
        default:
printf("invalid");
        }

                printf("\nPress y or Y to continue:");
                scanf("%s",&confirm);
                }while(confirm=='y'||confirm=='Y');

                return EXIT_SUCCESS;

        }
```

Recursion

A function that calls itself is known as a recursive function. And, this technique is known as recursion.

The C programming language supports recursion, that is, a function to call itself.

But, while using recursion, programmers need to be careful to define an exit condition from the function; otherwise, it will go into an infinite loop.

Recursive functions are very useful to solve many mathematical problems, such as calculating the factorial of a number and generating the Fibonacci series.

135. Write a program to find the power of given number using recursion.

```
#include <stdio.h>
/* Power function declaration */
double pow(double base, int expo);

int main()
{
    double base, power;
    int expo;

    /* Input base and exponent from user */
    printf("Enter base: ");
    scanf("%lf", &base);
    printf("Enter exponent: ");
    scanf("%d", &expo);

    // Call pow function
    power = pow(base, expo);
```

```
        printf("%.2lf ^ %d = %f", base, expo, power);

        return 0;
    }

    double pow(double base, int expo)
    {
        /* Base condition */
        if(expo == 0)
            return 1;
        else if(expo > 0)
            return base * pow(base, expo –1);
        else
            return 1 / pow(base, –expo);
    }
```

136. Write a program to display the Fibonacci series using recursion.

```
        #include <stdio.h>
        void getFibonacii(int a,int b, int n)
        {
            int sum;
            if(n>0)
            {
                sum=a+b;
                printf("%d ",sum);
                a=b;
                b=sum;
                getFibonacii(a,b,n–1);
            }
        }
        int main()
        {
            int a,b,sum,n;
            int i;

            a=0;        //first term
            b=1;        //second term

            printf("Enter total number of terms: ");
            scanf("%d",&n);

            printf("Fibonacii series is : ");
            //print a and b as first and second terms of series
            printf("%d\t%d\t",a,b);
```

```
        //call function with (n–2) terms
        getFibonacii(a,b,n–2);
        printf("\n");
        return 0;
}
```

137. Write a program to display the factorial of given number using recursion.

```
#include<stdio.h>

int fact(int n)
{
static int f=1;
        if(n==1)
         return 1;
        else
        f=n*fact(n–1);

return(f);
}
void main()
{
int n,f;
        printf("Enter a number");
        scanf("%d",&n);
        f=fact(n);
        printf("\nFactorial=%d",f);
}
```

12 . Pointer

A pointer is used in a C program to access the memory and manipulate the address or the value at address.

A pointer is a variable that contains the address in memory of another variable. We can have a pointer to any variable type.

The *unary* operator & gives the "address of a variable."

The *indirection* or dereference operator * gives the "contents of an object *pointed to* by a pointer."

Some C programming tasks are performed more easily with pointers, and other tasks, such as dynamic memory allocation, cannot be performed without using pointers.

A pointer is a variable whose value is the address of another variable, that is, direct address of the memory location.

Like any variable or constant, we must declare a pointer before using it to store any variable address.

datatype *pointer_variable_name;

Types of pointers in C are:

- **Null pointer**: A NULL pointer is a pointer that is pointing to nothing.
  int *ptr=NULL;

- **Dangling pointer**: A dangling pointer arises when an object is deleted or de-allocated, without modifying the value of the pointer, so that the pointer still points to the memory location of the de-allocated memory.
  char *ptr = malloc(Constant_Value);
  free (ptr); //ptr now becomes a dangling pointer

- **Generic pointers**: When a variable is declared as a pointer to type void, it is known as a generic pointer.
  int i; char c;
   void *the_data;
   i = 6; c = 'a';
   the_data = &I;
   the_data = &c;

Wild pointer:A pointer in C that has not been initialized till its first use is known as a wild pointer. A wild pointer points to some random memory location.

int *ptr;
// Ptr is a wild pointer, as it is not initialized Yet
printf("%d", *ptr);

138. Write a program to sort an array using a pointer.

```
#include <stdio.h>
void main()
{
  int *a,i,j,tmp,n,a1[100];

  printf(" Input the number of elements to store in the array : ");
  scanf("%d",&n);

  printf(" Input %d number of elements in the array : \n",n);
  for(i=0;i<n;i++)
    {
        printf(" element - %d : ",i+1);
        scanf("%d",&a1[i]);
        }
              a=a1;
  for(i=0;i<n;i++)
  {
  for(j=i+1;j<n;j++)
  {
    if( *(a+i) > *(a+j))
    {
    tmp = *(a+i);
    *(a+i) = *(a+j);
    *(a+j) = tmp;
    }
  }
  }
  printf("\n The elements in the array after sorting : \n");
  for(i=0;i<n;i++)
    {
        printf(" element - %d : %d \n",i+1,*(a+i));
    }
  printf("\n");
}
```

139. Write a program to find the greater number using a pointer and return the pointer.

```
#include <stdio.h>

int* findLarger(int*, int*);
void main()
{
int numa=0;
int numb=0;
int *result;

   printf(" Input the first number : ");
   scanf("%d", &numa);

   printf(" Input the second  number : ");
   scanf("%d", &numb);

result=findLarger(&numa, &numb);
printf(" The number %d is larger. \n\n",*result);
}

int* findLarger(int *n1, int *n2)
{
if(*n1 > *n2)
  return n1;
else
  return n2;
}
```

140. Write a program to generate the possible permutation of a given string.

```
#include<stdio.h>
#include<string.h>
void main()
{
   int n, i, k = 0 ;
   char a[10] ;
   void perm(char a[10], int k, int n) ;

   printf("Enter the string : ") ;
   scanf("%s", a) ;
   printf("\nThe permutation is :\n") ;
   n = strlen(a) ;
   perm(a, k, n) ;
}
```

```
void perm(char a[10], int k, int n)
{
    char t, d[10] ;
    int i ;
    if(k == n)
    {
        printf("\n%s", a) ;
        return ;
    }
    else
    {
        for(i = k ; i < n ; i++)
        {
            t = a[i] ;
            a[i] = a[k] ;
            a[k] = t ;
            strcpy(d, a) ;
            perm(d, k + 1, n) ;
        }
    }
}
```

141. Write a program to find the length of a given string usinga pointer.

```
#include <stdio.h>
int calculateLength(char*);

void main()
{
    char str1[25];
    int l;

    printf(" Input a string : ");
    gets(str1);

    l = calculateLength(str1);
    printf(" The length of the given string %s is : %d ", str1, l-1);
    printf("\n\n");

}

int calculateLength(char* ch) // ch = base address of array str1 (
&str1[0]  )
{
    int ctr = 0;
```

```
      while (*ch != '\0')
      {
        ctr++;
        ch++;
      }
      return ctr;
    }
```

141. Write a program to find the sum of elements of an array using a pointer.

```
#include <stdio.h>
void main()
{
  int arr1[10];
  int i,n, sum = 0;
  int *pt;

   printf(" Input the number of elements to store in the array
  (max 10) : ");
  scanf("%d",&n);

  printf(" Input %d number of elements in the array : \n",n);
  for(i=0;i<n;i++)
     {
        printf(" element - %d : ",i+1);
        scanf("%d",&arr1[i]);
        }

  pt = arr1; // pt store the base address of array arr1

  for (i = 0; i < n; i++) {
    sum = sum + *pt;
    pt++;
  }

  printf(" The sum of array is : %d\n\n", sum);
}
```

142. Write a program to print a given string in reverse order.

```c
#include <stdio.h>
int main()
{
  char str1[50];
  char revstr[50];
  char *stptr = str1;
  char *rvptr = revstr;
  int i=-1;

  printf(" Input a string : ");
  scanf("%s",str1);

  while(*stptr)
  {
   stptr++;
   i++;
  }
  while(i>=0)
  {
   stptr--;
   *rvptr = *stptr;
   rvptr++;
   --i;
  }
  *rvptr='\0';
  printf(" Reverse of the string is : %s\n\n",revstr);
  return 0;
}
```

11. Structure

A structure is a collection of variables of different types under a single name.

A structure is a user-defined data type in C language, which allows us to combine data of different types together.

A structure helps to construct a complex data type that is more meaningful. It is similar to an array, but an array holds data of similar type only.

By contrast, a structure can store data of any type, which is practically more useful.

Each element of a structure is called a member.

It works like a template in C++ and class in Java. You can have different type of elements in it.

It is widely used to store student information, employee information, product information, book information, and so on.

The syntax of a structure is:

```
struct name_of_structure
{members;}
```

To access the members of the structure, we write a variable name of the structure, followed by a dot(.) operator.

A structure can be nested inside another structure. In other words, the members of a structure can be of any other type including the structure.

Its syntax is:

```
structure tagname_1
{
    member1;
    member2;
    member3;
    ...
    membern;

    structure tagname_2
    {
        member_1;
        member_2;
```

```
        member_3;
        ...
        member_n;
      }, var1

} var2;
```

To access the members of the inner structure, we write a variable name of the outer structure, followed by a dot(.) operator, followed by the variable of the inner structure, followed by a dot(.) operator.

143. Write a program to create a structure "student,"access its members and display the details.

```
#include<stdio.h>
struct stu
{
        //member of structure
        char name[10];
        int age;
};
void main()
{
struct stu A,b; //variable of structure to access its member

printf("Enter name of student\n");
scanf("%s",A.name); // . Operator is used to access
member
printf("\nEnter age of student\n");
scanf("%d",&A.age);
printf("Enter name of student\n");
scanf("%s",b.name); // . Operator is used to access member
printf("\nEnter age of student\n");
scanf("%d",&b.age);

printf("\n%s is %d years old",A.name,A.age);
printf("\n%s is %d years old",b.name,b.age);
}
```

144. Write a program to create a structure and read data of 10 students.

```c
#include<stdio.h>
struct stu
{
        //member of structure
        char name[10];
        int age;
};
void main()
{
struct stu a[3];
        int i;
        for(i=0;i<3;i++)
        {
        printf("Enter name of student\n");
        scanf("%s",a[i].name);
        //. operator is used to access
        member
        printf("\nEnter age of student\n");
        scanf("%d",&a[i].age);

        }
        for(i=0;i<3;i++)
        {
        printf("\n%s is %d years old",a[i].name,a[i].age);
        }
}
```

145. Write a program to create a global variable of a structure and use it.

```c
#include<stdio.h>
struct stu
{
        char name[10];
        int age;
}s;
void main()
{
        printf("Enter name and age ");
        scanf("%s%d",s.name,&s.age);
        printf("\n%s is %d years old",s.name,s.age);
}
```

146. Write a program to create a structure using function.

```
#include<stdio.h>
struct stu
{
char n[10];
}s;
void read()
{
        printf("\nEnter name");
        scanf("%s",s.n);
}
void show()
{
        printf("\nHello %s",s.n);
}
void main()
{
        read();
        show();

}
```

147. Write a menu-driven program to read or write details of a structure "student."

```
#include<stdio.h>
#include<stdlib.h>

struct student
{
        char cou[10];
        float fee;
};
struct student read()
{
        struct student s;
        printf("\nEnter course and fee");
        scanf("%s%f",s.cou,&s.fee);
        return s;
}

void show(struct student s)
{
printf("\nstudent doing %s and paid fee %5.2f",s.cou,s.fee);
```

```
        }
        int main()
        {
                struct student s[100];
                int c,i=0,j;

                while(1)
                {
                printf("Enter choice:\nPress 1 for new record\nPress
                2 for display all\nPress any number for exit\n");
                scanf("%d",&c);
                switch(c)
                    {
                            case 1:
                                    s[i++]=read();
                                    system("cls"); //clears screen
                                    break;
                            case 2:
                                    for(j=0;j<i;j++)
                                    show(s[j]);
                                    break;
                                    default:
                                    exit(1);
                    }
                }
        return 0;
        }
```

148. Write a program to use a nested structure.

```
        #include<stdio.h>

        //Example of nested structure
        struct dates
        {
        int d,m,y;
        };
        struct stu
        {
                char name[10];
                struct dates dob,doj;
                float fee;
        };
```

```
void main()
{
struct stu a;
        printf("Enter name\n ");
        scanf("%s",a.name);
        printf("\nEnter date of birth\n");
        scanf("%d%d%d",&a.dob.d,&a.dob.m,&a.dob.y);
        printf("\nEnter date of joining\n");
        scanf("%d%d%d",&a.doj.d,&a.doj.m,&a.doj.y);
        printf("\nEnter fee\n");
        scanf("%f",&a.fee);
        printf("\n----Details---\n");
        printf("\nName:\t%s",a.name);
        printf("\nDOB:\t%d\\%d\\%d",a.dob.d,a.dob.m,a.dob.y);
        printf("\nDOJ:\t%d\\%d\\%d",a.doj.d,a.doj.m,a.doj.y);
        printf("\nFee:\t%5.2f",a.fee);

}
```

149. Write a program to created more than one nested structure.

```
#include<stdio.h>

struct dates
{
        int d,m,y;
};
struct student
{
                char name[20],course[20];
                struct dates dob,doj;
                float fee;
};
struct employee
{
                char name[20];
                struct dates dob,doj;
                float salary;
};
int main()
{
                struct student a;
                struct employee b;
                int c;
```

```
                              printf("enter choice 1 or 2");
                              scanf("%d",&c);
                              switch(c)
                              {
                              case 1:  printf("Enter name of student\n ");
                                       fflush(stdin);
                                       gets(a.name);

                                       printf("\nEnter date of birth\n");

                                       scanf("%d%d%d",&a.dob.d,&a.
                                       dob.m,&a.dob.y);
                                       printf("\nEnter date of joining\n");

                                       scanf("%d%d%d",&a.doj.d,&a.
                                       doj.m,&a.doj.y);
                                       printf("\nEnter course\n");

                                       scanf("%s",&a.course);
                                       printf("\nEnter fee\n");

                                       scanf("%f",&a.fee);

                                       printf("\n----Details---\n");
                                       printf("\nName:\t%s",a.name);
                                       printf("\nDOB:\t%d\\%d\\%d",a.
                                       dob.d,a.dob.m,a.dob.y);
                                       printf("\nDOJ:\t%d\\%d\\%d",a.doj.d,a.
                                       doj.m,a.doj.y);
                                       printf("\nCourse:\t%s",a.course);
                                       printf("\nFee:\t%5.2f",a.fee);
                                       break;
                 case 2:               printf("Enter name of employee\n ");
                                       scanf("%s",b.name);
                                       printf("\nEnter date of birth\n");
                                       scanf("%d%d%d",&b.dob.d,&b.
                                       dob.m,&b.dob.y);
                                       printf("\nEnter date of joining\n");
                                       scanf("%d%d%d",&b.doj.d,&b.
                                       doj.m,&b.doj.y);
                                       printf("\nsalary\n");
                                       scanf("%f",&b.salary);

                                       printf("\n----Details---\n");
```

```
                    printf("\nName:\t%s",b.name);
                    printf("\nDOB:\t%d\\%d\\%d",b.
                    dob.d,b.dob.m,b.dob.y);
                    printf("\nDOJ:\t%d\\%d\\%d",b.doj.d,b.
                    doj.m,b.doj.y);
                    printf("\nSalary:\t%5.2f",b.salary);
                    break;

                    default: printf("Invalid");
                    }

         }
```

Union

A union is a special datatype available in C,which allows to store different datatypes in the same memory location. We can define a union with many members, but only one member can contain a value at any given time.

Difference between a structure and union

	Structure	Union
Memory allocation	Members of structure do not share memory. So, a structure needs separate memory space for all its members, that is, all the members have unique storage.	A union shares the memory space among its members, so there is no need to allocate memory to all the members. Shared memory space is allocated, that is, equivalent to the size of member having largest memory.
Member access	Members of a structure can be accessed individually at any time.	At a time, only one member of union can be accessed.
Keyword	To define a structure, the *struct*keyword is used.	To define a union, the *union*keyword is used.
Initialization	*All* members of a structure can be initialized.	*Only* the *first* member of the union can be initialized.
Size	Size of the structure is $\geq$ to the sum of the each member's size.	Size of the union is equivalent to the size of the member having the *largest* size.

Syntax	struct struct_name { structure ele 1; structure ele 2; —————— —————— structure ele n; }struct_variable_name;	union union_name { union ele 1; union ele 2; —————— —————— union ele n; }union_variable_name;
Change in value	Change in the value of one member cannot affect the other in the structure.	Change in the value of one member can affect the value of other member.

150. Write a program to display the difference between a structure and union.

```c
#include<stdio.h>
struct info
{
char n[10];
int a;
};
union infor
{
char n[10];
int a;
};
void main()
{
        struct info i;
        union infor i1;

        printf("\nSizeof a=%d , n=%d,i is %d",sizeof(i.a),sizeof(
        i.n),sizeof(i));
        printf("\n\nSizeof a=%d , n=%d,i1 is %d",sizeof(i1.a),si
        zeof(i1.n),sizeof(i1));

        printf("\n\nEnter string and number");
        scanf("%s%d",i.n,&i.a);
        printf("\n\nStruct variable:%s\t%d",i.n,i.a);

        printf("\n\nEnter string and number");
        scanf("%s%d",i1.n,&i1.a);
        printf("\n\nunion variable:%s\t%d",i1.n,i1.a);

}
```

Typedef

typedef can be used to give a type a new name.

151. Write a program to display the use of a *typedef* statement.

```
#include<stdio.h>
void main()
{
typedef int myname;
myname  b=34;
printf("\nval=%d",b);
}
```

152. Write a program to display the use of a typedef statement in a structure.

```
#include<stdio.h>
Void main()
{
struct stu
{
        //member of structure
        char name[10];
        int age;
};
void main()
{
typedef struct stu student;
student a;
        printf("Enter name and age of student");
        scanf("%s%d",a.name,&a.age);
        printf("\n%s is %d years old",a.name,a.age);
}
```

153. Write a program to read and write data of a structure using a pointer.

```
#include<stdio.h>
struct student
{
        char course[10];
        float fee;
};
Void main()
{
Struct student *s;
```

```
Printf("enter course and fee of student");
Scanf("%s%f",s->course , &s->fee);

Printf("\nDetails of student\n");
Prrintf("She/he is doing %s and paid %f",s->course,s->fee);
}
```

154. Write a program to add two distances (feet–inch system) and display the result without the return statement.

```
#include <stdio.h>
struct distance
{
    int feet;
    float inch;
};
void add(struct distance d1,struct distance d2, struct distance
*d3);

int main()
{
    struct distance dist1, dist2, dist3;

    printf("First distance\n");
    printf("Enter feet: ");
    scanf("%d", &dist1.feet);
    printf("Enter inch: ");
    scanf("%f", &dist1.inch);

    printf("Second distance\n");
    printf("Enter feet: ");
    scanf("%d", &dist2.feet);
    printf("Enter inch: ");
    scanf("%f", &dist2.inch);

    add(dist1, dist2, &dist3);

    //passing structure variables dist1 and dist2 by value whereas
    passing structure variable dist3 by reference
    printf("\nSum of distances = %d\'-%.1f\'"", dist3.feet, dist3.
    inch);

    return 0;
```

```
}
void add(struct distance d1,struct distance d2, struct distance
*d3)
{
    //Adding distances d1 and d2 and storing it in d3
    d3->feet = d1.feet + d2.feet;
    d3->inch = d1.inch + d2.inch;

    if (d3->inch >= 12) {     /* if inch is greater or equal to 12,
converting it to feet. */
        d3->inch -= 12;
        ++d3->feet;
    }
}
```

13. Dynamic memory allocation

The process of allocating memory during program execution is called dynamic memory allocation.

Dynamic memory management refers to manual memory management. This allows us to obtain more memory when required and release it when not necessary.

Dynamic memory allocation funcytions in C are summarized in the following table:

Function	Syntax
malloc ()	malloc (number *sizeof(int));
calloc ()	calloc (number, sizeof(int));
realloc ()	realloc (pointer_name, number * sizeof(int));
free ()	free (pointer_name);
Function	Use of the function
malloc()	Allocates the requested size of bytes and returns a pointer the first byte of the allocated space
calloc()	Allocates space for an array's elements, initializes to zero, and then returns a pointer to memory
free()	De-allocates the previously allocated space
realloc()	Changes the size of previously allocated space

155. Write a program to use a structure's member through a pointer using the malloc() function.

```
#include <stdio.h>
#include <stdlib.h>
struct person    {
               int age;
               float weight;
               char name[30];
               };

int main()
{
   struct person *ptr;
   int i, num;
```

```
printf("Enter number of persons: ");
scanf("%d", &num);

ptr = (struct person*) malloc(num * sizeof(struct person));
// Above statement allocates the memory for n structures with
pointer person Ptr pointing to base address.

for(i = 0; i < num; ++i)
{
    printf("Enter name, age and weight of the person
    respectively:\n");
    scanf("%s%d%f", &(ptr+i)->name, &(ptr+i)->age, &(ptr+i)-
    >weight);
}

    printf("Displaying Infromation:\n");
    for(i = 0; i < num; ++i)
    printf("%s\t%d\t%.2f\n", (ptr+i)->name, (ptr+i)->age,
    (ptr+i)->weight);

    return 0;
}
```

156. Write a program to create memory for int, char, and float variables at runtime.

```
#include <stdio.h>
#include <stdlib.h>

int main()
{
    int *iVar;
    char *cVar;
    float *fVar;

    /*allocating memory dynamically*/

    iVar=(int*)malloc(1*sizeof(int));
    cVar=(char*)malloc(1*sizeof(char));
    fVar=(float*)malloc(1*sizeof(float));

    printf("Enter integer value: ");
    scanf("%d",iVar);

    printf("Enter character value: ");
    scanf(" %c",cVar);
```

```
        printf("Enter float value: ");
        scanf("%f",fVar);

        printf("Inputted value are: %d, %c, %.2f\
        n",*iVar,*cVar,*fVar);

        /*free allocated memory*/
        free(iVar);
        free(cVar);
        free(fVar);

        return 0;
}
```

157. Write a program to input and print a name using dynamic memory allocation.

```
        int main()
        {
            int n;
            char *name;

            printf("Enter limit of the text: ");
            scanf("%d",&n);

            /*allocate memory dynamically*/
            text=(char*)malloc(n*sizeof(char));

            printf("Enter text: ");
            scanf(" "); /*clear input buffer*/
            gets(name);

            printf("Inputted text is: %s\n",name);

            /*Free Memory*/
            free(name);

            return 0;
        }
```

158. Write a program to read a one D array, print the sum of all elements along with inputted array elements using dynamic memory allocation.

```
        #include <stdio.h>
        #include <stdlib.h>

        int main()
        {
```

```
int *arr;
int limit,i;
int sum=0;

printf("Enter total number of elements: ");
scanf("%d",&limit);

/*allocate memory for limit elements dynamically*/
arr=(int*)malloc(limit*sizeof(int));

if(arr==NULL)
{
   printf("Insufficient Memory, Exiting... \n");
   return 0;
}

printf("Enter %d elements:\n",limit);
for(i=0; i<limit; i++)
{
   printf("Enter element %3d: ",i+1);
   scanf("%d",(arr+i));
   /*calculate sum*/
   sum=sum + *(arr+i);
}

printf("Array elements are:");
for(i=0; i<limit; i++)
   printf("%3d ",*(arr+i));

printf("\nSum of all elements: %d\n",sum);

return 0;
}
```

159. Write a program to read and print the student details using a structure and dynamic memory allocation.

```
#include <stdio.h>
#include <stdlib.h>

/*structure declaration*/
struct student
{
   char name[30];
   int roll;
   float perc;
```

```
};
int main()
{
    struct student *st;

    /*Allocate memory dynamically*/
    st=(struct student*)malloc(1*sizeof(struct student));

    if(st==NULL)
    {
        printf("Insufficient Memory, Exiting... \n");
        return 0;
    }

    /*read and print details*/
    printf("Enter name: ");
    gets(st->name);
    printf("Enter roll number: ");
    scanf("%d",&st->roll);
    printf("Enter percentage: ");
    scanf("%f",&st->perc);

    printf("\nEntered details are:\n");
    printf("Name: %s, Roll Number: %d, Percentage: %.2f\n",st->name,st->roll,st->perc);

    return 0;
}
```

160. Write a program to allocate memory at runtime for an array.

```
#include <stdio.h>
#include <stdlib.h>
int main()
{
    int n,i,*p;
    printf("Enter number of elements: ");
    scanf("%d",&n);
    p=(int*)calloc(n, sizeof(int));
    if(p == NULL)
    {
        printf("memory cannot be allocated\n");
    }
    else
    {
```

```
      printf("Enter elements of array:\n");
      for(i=0;i<n;++i)
      {
        scanf("%d",&*(p+i));
      }
      printf("Elements of array are\n");
      for(i=0;i<n;i++)
      {
        printf("%d\n",*(p+i));
      }
    }
    return 0;
}
```

161. Write a program to use realloc.

```
#include <stdio.h>
#include <stdlib.h>
#include <string.h>
int main()
{
  char *p1;
  int m1, m2;
  m1 = 10;
  m2 = 20;
  p1 = (char*)malloc(m1);
  strcpy(p1, "Swati");
  p1 = (char*)realloc(p1, m2);
  strcat(p1, "Computers");
  printf("%s\n", p1);
  return 0;
}
```

14. File handling

File is a collection of bytes that are stored in secondary storage devices such as a disc. There are two types of files in a system. They are:

- Text files (ASCII)
- Binary files

Text files contain ASCII codes of digits, alphabets, and symbols.

Binary files contain collection of bytes (0s and 1s). Binary files are a compiled version of text files.

Basic file operations in C

The basic file operations in C are as follows:

1. Creating a new file (fopen with attributes as "a","a+", "w", or "w++").
2. Opening an existing file (fopen).
3. Reading from the file (fscanf or fgetc).
4. Writing to a file (fprintf or fputs).
5. Moving to a specific location in a file (fseek, rewind).
6. Closing a file (fclose).

    The syntax for the baic file operations is:

        FIIE *fp;

        Fp=fopen("Name of file", "mode");

Modes of operation in file are as follows:

- r: Opens a file in read mode and sets the pointer to the first character in the file. It returns null if the file does not exist.

- w: Opens a file in write mode. It returns null if the file could not be opened. If the file exists, data is overwritten.

- a: Opens a file in append mode. It returns null if the file does notopen.

- r+: Opens a file in read and write mode and sets the pointer to the first character in the file.

- w+: Opens a file in read and write mode and sets the pointer to the first character in the file. if the file to be opened does not exist, it gets created.

- a+: Opens a file in read and write mode and sets the pointer to the first character in the file. But, it cannot modify the existing contents.

File handling functions	Description
fopen ()	The fopen () function creates a new file or opens an existing file.
fclose ()	The fclose () function closes an opened file.
getw ()	The getw () function reads an integer from a file.
putw ()	The putw () function writes an integer to a file.
fgetc ()	The fgetc () function reads a character from a file.
fputc ()	The fputc () function writes a character to a file.
gets ()	The gets () function reads a line from the keyboard.
puts ()	The puts () function writes a line to the output screen.
fgets ()	The fgets () function reads a string from a file, one line at a time.
fputs ()	The fputs () function writes a string to a file.
feof ()	The feof () function finds the end of a file.
fgetchar ()	The fgetchar () function reads a character from the keyboard.
fprintf ()	The fprintf () function writes formatted data to a file.
fscanf ()	The fscanf () function reads formatted data from a file.
fputchar ()	The fputchar () function writes a character onto the output screen from the keyboard input.
fseek ()	The fseek () function moves the file pointer position to a given location.
SEEK_SET	SEEK_SET moves the file pointer position to the beginning of the file.
SEEK_CUR	SEEK_CUR moves the file pointer position to a given location.

SEEK_END	SEEK_END moves the file pointer position to the end of the file.
ftell ()	The ftell () function gives the current position of the file pointer.
rewind ()	The rewind () function moves the file pointer position to the beginning of the file.
getc ()	The getc () function reads a character from a file.
getch ()	The getch () function reads a character from the keyboard.
getche ()	The getche () function reads a character from the keyboard and echoes to the output screen.
getchar ()	The getchar () function reads a character from the keyboard.
putc ()	The putc () function writes a character to a file.
putchar ()	The putchar () function writes a character to the screen.
printf ()	The printf () function writes formatted data to the screen.
sprinf ()	The sprinf () function writes formatted output to a string.
scanf ()	The scanf () function reads formatted data from the keyboard.
sscanf ()	The sscanf () function reads formatted input from a string.
remove ()	The remove () function deletes a file.
fflush ()	The fflush () function flushes a file.

162. Write a program to open an existing file and read it character-by-character.

```c
#include<stdio.h>
void main()
{
FILE *fp,*fp1;
char c;

        fp=fopen("sz.c","r");
        if(fp==NULL)
         printf("\nFile does not exist");

        while(1)
        {
        c=fgetc(fp); //read char from sz.c

        if(c==EOF)
         break;
        printf("%c",c);
        }

        fclose(fp);
}
```

163. Write a program to copy an existing file.

```c
#include<stdio.h>
void main()
{
FILE *fp,*fp1;
char c;

        fp=fopen("sz.c","r");
        fp1=fopen("sz1.c","w");

        if(fp==NULL)
         printf("\nFile does not exist");

        while(1)
        {
        c=fgetc(fp); //read char from sz.c
        if(c==EOF)
         break;
        fputc(c,fp1); //write char into sz1.c
        //printf("%c",c);
        }
```

```
                printf("\nFile created");
                fclose(fp);
                fclose(fp1);
        }
```

164. Write a program to count the number of vowels in a given file.

```
        #include<stdio.h>
        int main()
        {
                FILE *fp;
                char c;
                int x=0;
                fp=fopen("sz1.c","r");
                while(1)
                {
                        c=fgetc(fp);
                        if(c==EOF)
                        break;
                        else if(c=='a'||c=='e'||c=='i'||c=='o'||c=='u')
                        x++;

                }
                        printf("\n%d",x);
                        fclose(fp);
                        return(0);
        }
```

165. Write a program to print names of all students from a file.

```
        #include<stdio.h>
        void main()
        {
        FILE *fp,*fp1;
        char name[10];
                fp=fopen("student_name.c","r");
                while(fgets(name,9,fp))
                {
                printf("%s",name);
                }
                fclose(fp);
        }
```

166. Write a program to input name of a student and update in an existing file.

```c
#include<stdio.h>
void main()
{
FILE *fp1;
char name[10
        fp1=fopen("student_name.c","a");

        printf("\nEnter ur name");
        gets(name);

        fputs(name,fp1); // write string into sz1.c

        printf("\nFile updated");

        fclose(fp1);
}
```

167. Write a program to create a copy of a file, but replace all *i* with *I*.

```c
#include<stdio.h>
void main()
{
        FILE *fp,*fp1;
        char c;
        fp=fopen("sz1.c","r");
        fp1=fopen("sz2.c","w");
        while(1)
        {
                c=fgetc(fp);
                if(c==EOF)
                break;
                else if(c=='i')
                c='I';
                fputc(c,fp1);

        }
        printf("\n File Created");
        fclose(fp);
        fclose(fp1);

}
```

168. Write a program to input data of students as a structure variable and write into a file.

```c
#include<stdio.h>
#include<conio.h>

struct stu
{
        //member of structure
        char name[10];
        int age;
        char phn[10];
};
void main()
{
        struct stu s;
        FILE *fp;
        fp=fopen("strct1.c","w");

        printf("Enter name of student\n");
        scanf("%s",s.name); // . Operator is used to
        access member

        printf("\nEnter age of student\n");
        scanf("%d",&s.age);
        fflush(stdin);
        printf("\nEnter phone");
        gets(s.phn);

        fwrite(&s,sizeof(s),1,fp);
        fclose(fp);
}
```

169. Write a program to read the structure variable from a file.

```c
#include<stdio.h>
#include<conio.h>

struct stu
{
        //member of structure
        char name[10];
        int age;
        char phn[10];
};
```

```
void main()
{
        struct stu s;
        FILE *fp;
        fp=fopen("strct1.c","r");

        fread(&s,sizeof(s),1,fp);

        printf("\nname=%s\tage=%d\tphone=%s",s.name,s.
age,s.phn);
        fclose(fp);
}
```

170. Write a program to read the file and store the lines into an array.

```
#include <stdio.h>
#include <stdlib.h>
#include <string.h>

#define LSIZ 128
#define RSIZ 10

int main(void)
{
   char line[RSIZ][LSIZ];
        char fname[20];
   FILE *fptr = NULL;
   int i = 0;
   int tot = 0;

        printf(" Input the filename to be opened : ");
        scanf("%s",fname);

   fptr = fopen(fname, "r");
   while(fgets(line[i], LSIZ, fptr))
        {
      line[i][strlen(line[i]) -1] = '\0';
      i++;
   }
   tot = i;
        printf("\n The content of the file %s  are : \n",fname);
   for(i = 0; i < tot; ++i)
   {
      printf(" %s\n", line[i]);
```

```
        }
        printf("\n");
        return 0;
}
```

171. Write a program to encrypt a file.

```
#include <stdio.h>
#include <stdlib.h>

void main()
{
        char fname[20], ch;
        FILE *fp, *fp1;

        printf(" Input the name of file to encrypt : ");
        scanf("%s",fname);

        fp=fopen(fname, "r");
        if(fp==NULL)
        {
                printf(" File does not exists or error in
                opening..!!");
                exit(1);
        }
        Fp1=fopen("temp.txt", "w");
        if(fp1==NULL)
        {
                printf(" Error in creation of file temp.txt ..!!");
                fclose(fp);
                exit(2);
        }
        while(1)
        {
                ch=fgetc(fp);
                if(ch==EOF)
                {
                        break;
                }
                else
                {
                        ch=ch+100;
                        fputc(ch, fp1);
                }
```

```
          }
          fclose(fp);
          fclose(fp1);
          fp=fopen(fname, "w");
          if(fp==NULL)
          {
                    printf(" File does not exists or error in
opening..!!");
                    exit(3);
          }
          Fp1=fopen("temp.txt", "r");
          if(fp1==NULL)
          {
                    printf(" File does not exists or error in
opening..!!");
                    fclose(fp);
                    exit(4);
          }
          while(1)
          {
                    ch=fgetc(fp1);
                    if(ch==EOF)
                    {
                              break;
                    }
                    else
                    {
                              fputc(ch, fp);
                    }
          }
          printf(" File %s successfully encrypted ..!!\n\n", fname);
          fclose(fp);
          fclose(fp);
}
```

172. Write a program to decrypt a file.

```c
#include <stdio.h>
#include <stdlib.h>

void main()
{
        char ch, fname[20];
        FILE *fp, *fp1;

        printf(" Input the name of file to decrypt : ");
        scanf("%s",fname);
        fp=fopen(fname, "w");
        if(fp==NULL)
        {
                printf(" File does not exists or error in
                opening..!!");
                exit(7);
        }
        fp1=fopen("temp.txt", "r");
        if(fp1==NULL)
        {
                printf(" File does not exists or error in
                opening..!!");
                fclose(fp);
                exit(9);
        }
        while(1)
        {
                ch=fgetc(fp1);
                if(ch==EOF)
                {
                        break;
                }
                else
                {
                        ch=ch-100;
                        fputc(ch, fp);
                }
        }
        printf(" The file %s decrypted successfully..!!\n\
        n",fname);
```

```
            fclose(fp);
            fclose(fp1);

    }
```

173. Write a program to display use of enum.

```
    #include <stdio.h>

    enum course {C,JAVA,VB,HTML,JS};

    int main()
    {
        enum course cou;
        cou = JAVA;
        printf("course is %d",cou+1);
        return 0;
    }
```

174. Write a program to display the use of sprintf().

```
    #include <stdio.h>

    int main()
    {
        char str[20];
            char course[10];
            float fee,f;
        printf("enter course and fee");
            scanf("%s%f",course,&fee);

            sprintf(str,"%s:%f",course,fee);
            puts(str);

        return 0;
    }
```

175. Write a program to display the use of sscanf().

```
    #include <stdio.h>
    int main ()
    {
        char buffer[30]="Swati Computers ";
        char First[20],Second[10];
        sscanf (buffer,"%s %s",First,Second);
```

```
            printf (" %s - %s \n",First,Second);
            return 0;
        }
```

176. Write a program to displaythe use of getch(),putch(), getchar(), putchar(),
gets(), and puts().

```
#include <stdio.h>
#include<conio.h>
int main ()
{
    char ch,str[50];

            printf("Enter a character");
            ch=getch();
            printf("\nU have input:");
            putch(ch);

            printf("\n\nEnter a character");
            ch=getchar();

            printf("u have input:");
            putchar(ch);

            fflush(stdin);

            printf("\n\nEnter a string");
            gets(str);

            printf("u have input:");
            puts(str);

        return 0;
    }
```

15. Bitwise operators

- Bitwise operators are used to perform bit operations.

  Decimal values are converted into binary values, which are the sequence of bits, and bitwise operators work on these bits.

- Bitwise operators in the C language are & (bitwise AND), | (bitwise OR), ~ (bitwise NOT), ^ (XOR), << (left shift), and >> (right shift).

Truth table for bitwise operations and bitwise operators.

First Value	Second value	AND	OR	XOR
0	0	0	0	0
0	1	0	1	1
1	0	0	1	1
1	1	1	1	0

There are two bitwise shift operators. They are:

- Right shift (>>)
- Left shift (<<)

177. Write a program to use the bitwise AND (&) operator.

```
#include <stdio.h>
#include<conio.h>
int main ()
{
int a = 12, b = 25;
    printf("Output = %d", a&b);
return 0;
}
```

Explanation:

```
12 = 00001100 (in Binary)
25 = 00011001 (in Binary)

Bit operation of 12 and 25
  00001100
& 00011001
  _____
  00001000 = 8 (in decimal)
```

178. Write a program to use the bitwise OR (|) operator.

```
#include <stdio.h>
#include<conio.h>
int main ()
{
int a = 12, b = 25;
    printf("Output = %d", a|b);
return 0;
}
```

Explanation:

12 = 00001100 (in Binary)
25 = 00011001 (in Binary)

Bitwise OR operation of 12 and 25
  00001100
  00011001
  _____
  00011101 = 29 (in decimal)

179. Write a program to use the bitwise XOR (^) operator.

```
#include <stdio.h>
#include<conio.h>
int main ()
{
int a = 12, b = 25;
    printf("Output = %d", a^b);
return 0;
}
```

Explanation:

12 = 00001100 (in Binary)
25 = 00011001 (o=in Binary)
Bitwise XOR operation of 12 and 25
  00001100
  00011001
  _____
  00010101 = 21 (in decimal)

180. Write a program to use the bitwise complement operator (~).

```
#include <stdio.h>
#include<conio.h>
int main ()
```

```
{
int b = 35;
    printf("Output = %d", ~b);
return 0;
}
```

Explanation:

35 = 00100011 (in Binary)

Bitwise complement operation of 35
~ 00100011
_____
11011100 = 220 (in decimal)

182. Write a program to use shift operators.

```
#include <stdio.h>
int main()
{
    int num=212, i;
    for (i=0; i<=2; ++i)
        printf("Right shift by %d: %d\n", i, num>>i);

    printf("\n");

    for (i=0; i<=2; ++i)
        printf("Left shift by %d: %d\n", i, num<<i);

    return 0;
}
```

Explanation:

212 = 11010100 (in binary)
212>>2 = 00110101 (in binary) [right-shift by two bits]
212 = 11010100 (in binary)
212<<1= 110101000 (in binary) [left-shift by one bit]

16. Miscellaneous

Enum

Enumeration (or enum) is a user-defined datatype in C. It is mainly used to assign names to integral constants, the names make a program easy to read, and maintain.

```c
#include <stdio.h>

enum course {C,JAVA,VB,HTML,JS};

int main()
{
    enum course cou;
    cou = JAVA;
    printf("course is %d",cou+1);
    return 0;
}
```

Header files

A header file in the C programming language is a file with .h extension,which contains a set of common function declarations and macro definitions that can be shared across multiple program files.

The C language provides a set of in-built header files that contain commonly used utility functions and macros.

Types of header files in C

- .User-defined header files.
- In-built header files

The syntaxes of a header file are:

```c
#include <Header_file_name>
```
```c
#include "Header_file_name"
```

C standard library header file

<assert.h>	**Conditionally compiled macro that compares its argument with zero**
<complex.h> (since C99)	Complex number arithmetic
<ctype.h>	Functions to determine the type contained in the character data
<errno.h>	Macros reporting error conditions
<fenv.h> (since C99)	Floating-point environment
<float.h>	Limits of float types
<inttypes.h> (since C99)	Format conversion of integer types
<iso646.h> (since C95)	Alternative operator spellings
<limits.h>	Sizes of basic types
<locale.h>	Localization utilities
<math.h>	Common mathematics functions
<setjmp.h>	Non-local jumps
<signal.h>	Signal handling
<stdalign.h> (since C11)	Alignas and alignof convenience macros
<stdarg.h>	Variable arguments
<stdatomic.h> (since C11)	Atomic types
<stdbool.h> (since C99)	Boolean type
<stddef.h>	Common macro definitions
<stdint.h> (since C99)	Fixed-width integer types
<stdio.h>	Input/output
<stdlib.h>	General utilities: memory management, program utilities, string conversions, and random numbers

<stdnoreturn.h> (since C11)	noreturn convenience macros
<string.h>	String handling
<tgmath.h> (since C99)	Type-generic math (macros wrapping math.h and complex.h)
<threads.h> (since C11)	Thread library
<time.h>	Time/date utilities
<uchar.h> (since C11)	UTF-16 and UTF-32 character utilities
<wchar.h> (since C95)	Extended multibyte and wide character utilities
<wctype.h> (since C95)	Functions to determine the type contained in the wide character data

Macro- and preprocessor in C

In a C program, all lines starting with a hash (#) are processed by a preprocessor that is a special program invoked by the compiler. In a very basic term, preprocessor takes a C program and produces another C program without any #.

The following are some interesting facts about preprocessors in C:

1. When we use the include directive, the contents of included header file (after preprocessing) are copied to the current file.

Angular brackets < and > instruct the preprocessor to look in the standard folder where all header files are held.

Double quotes "and" instruct the preprocessor to look into the current folder, and if the file is not present in the current folder, then it looks in the standard folder of all header files.

2. When we use define for a constant, the preprocessor generates a C program where the defined constant is searched, and matching tokens are replaced with the given expression.

In the C programming language, the #define directive allows the definition of macros within the source code.

These macro definitions allow constant values to be declared for use throughout the code.

Macro definitions are not variables and cannot be changed by our program code, like variables.

We generally use this syntax when creating constants that represent numbers, strings, or expressions.

The syntax for #define is:

>   #define Constant_name value

>   #define Constant_name (Expression)

Some are #if, #elif, #else, and #endif directives.

The #if directive, with the #elif, #else, and #endifdirectives, controls compilation of portions of a source file.

If the expression we write (after the #if) has a non-zero value, the line group immediately following the #if directive is retained in the translation unit.

17. Extra questions

1. What arethe outputs of the following programs?
```
#include <stdio.h>
using namespace std;
int main()
{
    int a = 21;
    int c ;
    c = a++;
    printf("%d",c);
    return 0;
}
```
    Answer: 21

2. ```
#include <stdio.h>
using namespace std;
int main()
{
    int x = 5, y = 5;
        Printf("%d %d",++x,--y;
            return 0;
    }
```
    Answer: 6 4

3. ```
int main()
{
    int x = 5, y = 5, z;
    x = ++x; y = --y;
    z = x++ + y--;
    printf("%d",z);
    return 0;
}
```

    Answer: 10

4. int main()
   {
       int num1 = 5;
       int num2 = 3;
       int num3 = 2;
       num1 = num2++;
       num2 = --num3;
       printf("%d %d %d",num1,num2,num3);

       return 0;
   }
           Answer: 3 1 1

5. #include <stdio.h>
   int main()
   {
       int a = 1, b = 1, c;
       c = a++ + b;
       printf("%d, %d", a, b);
   }
           Answer: a=2 , b=1

6. void main(){
   int i=5,j=10,num;
   num=(++i,++j,i+j);
   printf("%d %d %d",num,i,j);
   }

           Answer: 17 6 11

7. void main()
   {
   int i=5;
   printf("%d",i+++++i);
   }
           Answer: Compiler error

8. int main()
```
{
    FILE *fp1, *fp2;
    fp1=fopen("file.c", "w");
    fp2=fopen("file.c", "w");
    fputc('A', fp1);
    fputc('B', fp2);
    fclose(fp1);
    fclose(fp2);
    return 0;
}
```
Answer: B

9. int main()
```
{
    int k=1;
    printf("%d == 1 is " "%s\n", k, k==1?"TRUE":"FALSE");
    return 0;
}
```
Answer : 1=1 is TRUE

10. char *str = "char *str = %c%s%c; main(){ printf(str, 34, str, 34);}";
    void main()
```
{
        printf(str, 34, str, 34);
}
```

Answer: char *str = "char *str = %c%s%c; main()
                { printf(str, 34, str, 34);}"; main(){ printf(str, 34, str, 34);}

11. int main()
```
{
    float a=3.15529;
    printf("%2.1f\n", a);
    return 0;
}
```
Answer: 3.2

12. int main()
{
  char *p;
  p="%d\n";
  p++;
  p++;
  printf(p–2, 23);
  return 0;
}
      Answer: 23

13. int main()
    {
      printf("%%%%\n");
      return 0;
    }
      Answer: %%

14. int main()
    {
      FILE *ptr;
      char i;
      ptr = fopen("myfile.c", "r");
      while((i=fgetc(ptr))!=NULL)
        printf("%c", i);
      return 0;
    }
      Answer: infinite loop

15. int main()
    {
      int a=100;
      printf("%1d\n", a);
      return 0;
    }
      Answer: 100

16. void main()
    {
    int i,j;
    printf("%d %d\n", scanf("%d", &i),scanf("%d",&j));
    }
      Answer: 1 1

17. What is the purpose of "rb" in the fopen() function used in the following code?
    FILE *fp;
    fp = fopen("source.txt", "rb");
        Answer : open "source.txt" in binary mode for reading

18. int main()
    {
    char *str;
    str="%s";
    printf(str,"s");
    }
        Answer: S

19. Write output of the following:
    Assuming that the array begins at the location 1002 and the size of an integer
    is 4 bytes.
    void main()
    {
    Int a[3][4]={1,2,3,4,5,6,7,8,9,10,11,12};
    Printf("%u %u %u",a[0]+1,*{a[0]+1),*(*(a+0)+1));
    }
        Answer: 1006 2 2

20. void main()
    {
    Char str1[20]="Swati", str2[20]="Computers";
    Printf("%s",strcpy(str2,strcat(str1,str2)));
    }
        Answer: SwatiComputers

21. void main()
    {
    printf(5+"good morning");
    }
        Answer: morning

22. void main()
    {
    char str[] ="Jai\0Bharat\0";
    printf("%s",str);
    }
        Answer: Jai

23. void main()
    {
    Printf("%d %d %d", sizeof(3.0f), sizeof('3'),sizeof(3.0));
    }
        Answer: 4 2 8

24. void main()
    {
                printf("%c\n", 7["SwatiComputers"]);
    }
        Answer: m

25. int main()
    {
        char str[] = "peace";
        char *s = str;
        printf("%s\n", s++ +3);
        return 0;
    }
        Answer: ce

26. int main() {

                int m = –10, n = 20;
                n = (m < 0) ? 0 : 1;
                printf("%d %d", m, n);

                }
        Answer: –10 0

www.ingramcontent.com/pod-product-compliance
Lightning Source LLC
LaVergne TN
LVHW022318060326

832902LV00020B/3541